How to Increase Your Child's Verbal Intelligence

HOW TO INCREASE YOUR CHILD'S VERBAL INTELLIGENCE

The Language Wise Method

GEOFFREY McGUINNESS

CARMEN McGUINNESS

Yale University Press

New Haven and London

Designed by and set in type by Carmen and Geoffrey McGuinness.

Printed in the United States of America.

Library of Congress catalogue card number: 99-066923

ISBN: 0-300-08318-1 (cloth : alk. paper) — 0-300-08320-3 (pbk. : alk. paper)

A catalogue record for this book is available from the British Library.

The paper in this book meets the guidelines for permanence and durability of the Committee on Production Guidelines for Book Longevity of the Council on Library Resources.

10   9   8   7   6   5   4   3   2   1

Dedicated to

Swen Nater—once inspired by us is now a
giant inspiration to us all.

CONTENTS

PREFACE

When we established Read America in 1993 and set to the task of uncovering the mystery of reading, our intention was to put an end to the pendulum swings that had left generations of children without the skills they needed to read and understand what they had read. It was obvious to us that decoding was our point of departure. If you can't decode the words on the page, there is no chance of gaining meaning. However, we also knew from considerable research in the field that after the ability to segment sounds in words, one of the phonological processing skills taught at the Read America clinic, verbal intelligence is the highest correlator to comprehension. According to one such study done at the University of Texas at Austin (Juel, et al, Acquisition of Literacy, *Journal of Educational Psychology*, 1986), segmenting and intelligence are the *only* correlates to reading *and* oral comprehension. Once good segmenting skills are established, intelligence is the only remaining variable that mitigates both written and oral comprehension. Numerous other studies have investigated those aspects of intelligence which specifically correlate to oral and reading comprehension and revealed them to be vocabulary, logical reasoning and creativity—verbal intelligence.

With this knowledge, we set to the task of dealing with the first issue of reading—decoding. The result was Phono-Graphix, a method of teaching the skills needed for decoding and encoding the English orthographic code. Our goal was to make this method as quick as possible without sacrificing effectiveness, so that there would be instructional time remaining to move on to comprehension was realized early in 1995 when we had completed the study that was to be published in the *Orton Annals of Dyslexia*. We were stunned by our success. Since then the popularity of our clinical program, launched by the Orton Annals study released in 1996, has grown as has the spread of *Phono-Graphix Word Work*, a curriculum and materials for applying the method in schools, and *Reading Reflex*, a book for parents and teachers released by Free Press in February, 1998, and by Penguin in Great Britain August, 1998. There are now over one-hundred-fifty Phono-Graphix trainers training teachers in the US, Great Britain, the Republic of Ireland, Australia, New Zealand and South Africa. Media reports of the success of Phono-Graphix have appeared in newspapers and on television across the English speaking world.

With this accomplished, we moved on to our next quest, verbal intelligence. Until parents and teachers understand what comprehension is, and are given an effective way of improving it, only half the story has been told, only half the job done. So moving on to our second challenge, we set to work in 1995 to create a method of augmenting those aspects of intelligence that are known to improve the ability to *understand* what one has read or heard—comprehension. As we did with decoding, we began with a look at the history of instructional methods. Over the decades since compulsory education, many fads and trends have been interwoven with rote drill and formularized instruction intended to leave the child with the skills necessary to understand what she read or heard and to be able to put her ideas down on paper. Rote vocabulary building activities have included drills such as writing the word three times and then copying the first entry dictionary definition. Comprehension has been synonymous with , 'who', 'what', 'when' and 'where', with 'why' sometimes appearing as a bonus question. Writing activities centered around a five step formula for creating the perfect paragraph. In recent years the trends and fads have begun to win over the rote drills and formulas in the battle for comprehension and expression instruction. Many educators came to doubt the efficacy of the old drills and came to fear that what they in fact teach is memorization of arbitrary 'big' words, 'rules' for how many words a sentence must have to avoid being a fragment or risk being a run-on, and mnemonics or other 'tricks' for passing the quiz.

Since the birth of whole language in 1980, the formularized methods have clearly lost the war for dominion over comprehension instruction. It was at about that time that terms like 'critical reasoning' and 'creative thinking' started to appear on content inventories and student assessment forms. When inquiring teachers like these authors asked what that meant, they were led to leather bound volumes with newly inserted passages like this one, "...the ability to predict what might happen in a story", as taken from a Lee County, Florida school district document, *Guidelines For Curriculum Content*. What school district officials apparently didn't have the verbal prowess to realize when they drafted this guideline was that it is fallacious by definition. One cannot *predict*, or "make known before" (Webster) what *might* happen. One can *presume*, "suppose or venture" about what *might* happen, but by definition, one can only predict or fail to predict what *will* happen. Clearly the authors of this guideline lacked a fundamental grasp of the meaning of the key words involved in resolving this logical inconsistency, which lead them to draft an exposition which is incomprehensible, the very problem they sought to avoid for their young students. And while one is examining the vocabulary of this goal, one might go on to ask the question, what would _uncritical_ reasoning look like? Maybe that's what the kids mean when they say, "whatever". Isn't it ironic that the very students who were reared on these 'critical reasoning' activities would develop such highly _uncritical_ slang. In short, our historical review left us disappointed though not surprised to learn that the only new things whole language had brought to comprehension instruction were new tricks for remembering. Understanding was still something that stood apart and was assumed to follow if only we could remember long enough.

According to studies like Report Card on the Nation and States, the 1995 STATS Canada study and The National Adult Literacy Survey, none of the above is working. The first study revealed that an astronomical 43% of the nation's children are below basic competency in reading, while the 1995 STATS Canada study and The Adult Literacy Survey reveal that Americans rank second from the bottom among twelve countries in prose and document literacy. In each age group studied, Americans ranked the lowest among all nations at the skills of understanding and using information in text. When looked at across age groups, each of the other countries shows improvement from the oldest to the youngest group, showing that these countries have become more literate over the years, while Americans have gotten less literate over the years. *Language Wise* is a program that addresses the issues. It directly trains the variables of verbal intelligence that have been shown to correlate to oral and reading comprehension, as well as exposition. With average reading comprehension gains of four years, two months on the Peabody Individual Achievement Test (PIAT-r) reading comprehension sub-test, *Language Wise* offers a new paradigm. It offers the notion that to make children understand better, you must make them smarter—more *language wise*. Are parents and teachers ready for such a paradigm?

In our travels around the US and Great Britain, training teachers in the Phono-Graphix decoding method, we've heard many haunting questions that lead us to believe that parents and teachers are indeed ready. The most compelling came from a teacher in Philadelphia—Edie. Like most teachers we train, Edie praised Phono-Graphix. Then she asked an important question. "Once a child has learned to read, is there anything that I can do to help him better understand what he has read?" She went on to say, "I know the things I do won't hurt my students, but do they actually help them?" Consider this—the question really is, *"Can I make my students smarter?"* Can you imagine going to work each day not even knowing if anything you do is having any effect at all?—knowing only that it isn't hurting anyone? As often happens when fate is having its way with you, Edie's question came to us again, but this time from a parent attending a talk we gave in Tallahassee, Florida, "I've read every parenting book I could get my hands on in the last eight years. The more I read, the less I know. Maybe *you* can answer my question. Is intelligence set or can a parent enhance it?" These questions stun us. They are like fingernails on the blackboard of the conscience. They are in sum a plea, "Tell us we are needed for something more than 'behavior management' and 'quality time'." I'm reminded of a phenomenon I've experienced and observed many times—I'll call it the 'futility effect'. It's what happens when you're searching for some misplaced item, usually keys or a wallet. You're not sure that it's even remotely nearby. The last time this happened to me it was my new sunglasses that I sought. My dog Sophie was leashed and waiting impatiently for her morning walk. I was rifling through the regular places—purse, briefcase, pockets, kitchen 'catch all' drawer, but all the while, I had it in my head that Mandy (my fourteen year old) might have borrowed the glasses. Stricken by the 'futility effect' I didn't find them. When Mandy got home from school I asked her if she'd seen my glasses. "Yeah Mom, they're in your purse. I saw them when I got my lunch money." And indeed they were.

Are parents and teachers suffering from the 'futility effect'? Do they set about the task of raising and educating America's most precious resource with disbelief standing between them and the object of their efforts? *Language Wise* is a book that will say, **"Yes, it is there. You can make your children and students better understand what they read and hear. Here is the mountain of evidence that it can be done and here's how to do it."** We are entering a period in reading instruction in which the pencils have all been sharpened and the statistical calculators have all been stocked with new batteries. It was the data that ended the game and it is the data that will lead the way to the new game. We know, from thirty years of research, a great deal about how language is processed, how children develop schema based upon what they read or hear, how children communicate and build vocabulary, how children create their world each day through structures of meaning. *Language Wise* is a book that addresses these issues and goes on to build an inventory of goals and a catalog of activities for the achievement of these goals. The premise is a simple one which speaks to every parent who has ever had aspirations for their child, every teacher who has ever entered the classroom hoping to make a difference—make the child more verbally intelligent and the child will be better at comprehension and exposition. Language, as all things do, has a nature. It is by nature symbolic. Its symbolism is multi-dimensional. Help your child to understand the multi-dimensional symbolic nature of language, give her valid opportunities to practice receiving and sending these symbols and she will become a master of her language, her medium of thought. *Language Wise* is laced with the stories of real parents and children—parents who, like all parents, hoped for the best for their children but were afraid to seek it for fear it might not be there. Acceptance was their motto as they set about the task of raising average children—until Read America's *Language Wise* program forever changed the possibilities. As with our Phono-Graphix reading method, Read America's goal is to put the information in the hands of those who care the most, parents and teachers. It's time to move beyond, "How did you do it? How did you make David interested in history?... literature?... science?" to, "Yes, *I* can do it. *I* can make my child smarter, more motivated, more creative, more *Language Wise*."

The book is laid out in two sections. Section one contains six chapters. Chapter one reveals the nature of verbal intelligence and focuses on the need for the book. Chapter two reveals the nature of language and vocabulary. Chapter three discusses language acquisition and developmental expectations. Chapter four addresses attention and memory. Chapter five illustrates the part of logical reasoning and creativity in verbal intelligence. Each chapter is laced with the stories of real youngsters. Section two contains the lessons and activities of the *Language Wise* program.

—Geoffrey & Carmen McGuinness

CHAPTER ONE

VERBAL INTELLIGENCE
CAN I MAKE MY CHILD MORE "LANGUAGE WISE"?

As you open this book, and read the words written on this page, you use one of man's greatest inventions—written language. To understand the information on these pages you will use what we call verbal intelligence—the aspects of intelligence that enable you to understand and use spoken and written language. While reading these pages you'll sort through information, categorizing it into types. Your categories may vary from those established by another reader. You may categorize information you need to know right now as opposed to information that can wait until your child is a little older. Or, you may categorize based on what you agree with versus what you don't agree with. Still another reader may sort through what he already knows about language and verbal intelligence, separating it from what is new. Categorizing is, in a sense, comparison and contrast. You take in information about a topic, compare it to prior information, contrast what doesn't compare, and sort into categories.

While categorizing, you'll use logic to reason through the words. If on the next page I suggest that the best way to assure that your child is gifted in language is to bathe him in the juice of two mangoes twice weekly, you will evoke your knowledge of how the world works, your knowledge about language and about children and about mangoes, and you will determine that this suggestion is illogical—that it doesn't work within the constraints of the things we're dealing with, kids, language and mangoes.

You'll also use inference, based on prior knowledge. So when I explain that ten year old Bobby tended to be more interested in the Bulls than his home work, you'll infer that he's a basketball fan—and a typical ten year old male.

While categorizing and applying logic, inferring, comparing and contrasting you'll be building a schema, or a theory based on what you read and what you already know. When you build a schema or theory about something you 'know' it in your own terms. You no longer have to 'remember' all the elements or parts of the information. They have become part of a larger structure that is your schema. The very word 'information' implies this process of schema formation—in-form-ation—to form within.

If you're a creative thinker you may even make some leaps, reorganizing the basic parts of the information in new ways.

To do all of this, you will of course need to be familiar with the vocabulary I use and the relationship of one word to another. So when I talk about the "child learning" you will understand what a "child" is and that "learning" is something he does, and what that something is.

Later, after reading this book, you'll use expressive skills to discuss it with others, maybe your spouse or a colleague. You won't have to recall everything we wrote on every page to do this. You'll choose just the right words to convey the gist of the book to those who you wish to share it with. If your listener questions you on a particular aspect of the book, you'll be able to offer more detail in that area, perhaps an analogy or an example.

The ability to do all of this is what we mean when we speak of verbal intelligence. It is *the ability to understand, make judgments about, store, retrieve and talk about what we think, hear or read.* Fifty percent of the content of intelligence tests measure language based abilities just such as these. Yet very little of this is actually taught in schools. And almost none of it is taught with an eye toward increasing I.Q.

Making Your Child Language Wise

When we learn we are about to be graced with a child, many thoughts pass through our minds. The first concern is health, and for many, the expenses associated with the new child. There's a list of paraphernalia to acquire. High chair, crib, play pen and bassinet are all purchased and in place before baby arrives.

Once he does arrive, and health is established, other concerns take precedence. When will baby sleep through the night, roll over, sit up, take his first step, speak his first word, learn to drink from a cup, eat with a spoon? These first accomplishments seem basic, but actually reflect so much about us as human creatures. The abilities to move about on two legs, to use utensils and to speak establish strong boundaries between us and much of the rest of the animal kingdom. These skills in combination denote us as intelligent, independent humans.

The amount of time that goes into the teaching of a human child is remarkably long compared to the teaching of a cat or a panda bear who is born with many innate skills and instincts. While the infant cat knows much about things like grooming himself, the human child has very little in the way of useful instincts, and must be taught most of what he must know to get along in the human world. The human parent works at raising the human child for as many as twenty years before the child is considered independent and mature—ready for life without the parent. Potentially this effort will be well rewarded. Even the most clever cat is little competition to the human child, who may one day write a great novel, save the free world from fascism, develop a new system of economic analysis, compose a musical masterpiece, invent a new form of space travel, cure cancer, or devise a system for transforming iron into gold. But do we spend enough time engaged in active language instruction, or do we stop fretting once baby can talk, leaving the rest to natural development, the school and chance?

Nature or Nurture—Can I Make My Child Smarter?

To give your child the best chance in life you won't leave much to chance. The quantity and quality of a child's education are critically important to the outcome. The more instruction he receives and the higher the quality, the more likely he will reach independence, and with a bit of luck, accomplish something great. We don't mean to play down the importance of the natural skills that your child brings to his education. If your child is naturally gifted in mathematics he will be more likely to be selected for the last remaining spot in the architectural college of his choice. Also affecting the outcome are his individual ambitions, motives and drives. If he wants more than his next breath to be an architect, and has strong ambitions and drives, he will be more likely to learn with difficulty the mathematical skills that nature didn't offer with ease. But regardless of whether these skills come easily or require mammoth personal drive and commitment, once he has learned them he'll be smarter. So what's a parent to do? Will all your efforts pay off? What extent does fate play on whether your child writes a Nobel Prize winning novel?

According to a 1948 landmark intelligence study (Honzik, McFarlane and Allen), intelligence scores can vary as much as 50 points from the age of six to eighteen, with fifteen percent of the population experiencing changes of fifteen points or more. Apparently nature graces each of us with a range of potential, probably based upon genealogy, prenatal care, and birth conditions, and then nurture enhances or detracts from this, giving or taking as many as 50 points.

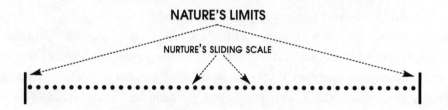

In this study, the highest correlate to increase in intelligence was consistent parental concern with educational achievement. This finding was backed up in a 1988 National Educational Longitudinal Study, which indicated that the schools with the highest student achievement were those with the highest parental involvement. This finding held up across socio-economic strata. The story of one Read America client exemplifies this very well. Brinnae was the seventeen year old daughter of a lawyer dad and a newspaper reporter mom. "Brinnae was such a bright kid," her father reflected at our intake appointment. "We never expected her to take such a downward slide." Brinnae's story is not uncommon. At seventeen her I.Q. score was 109. "I was really trying to do well," Brinnae told the test giver after the test. Six years earlier, at age twelve, Brinnae's I.Q. score was 132, a sizable difference from her comparatively modest 109 score leaving high school. In Brinnae's case, this "slide" as her father called it, kept her from being accepted into the college of her choice—the college from which her dad and his dad had each received a juris doctor. Brinnae's parents confessed that they had made few demands on Brinnae during her secondary education. "We placed her in a good school and assumed she would do the work," her mother explained. "We should have expected more of her."

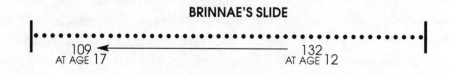

In another study (McCall, 1973), increases in individual intelligence oc-curred when the child was deliberately trained in skills that were not yet essen-tial.   We've had many such students pass through our doors at Read America—one such student was seven year old Danny. It was a challenge even scheduling Danny's *Language Wise* therapy. His life was filled with educational enrichment. Monday, Wednesday and Friday were piano lessons. On Wednesday he went from his piano lesson directly to his Spanish tutor, who he also saw on Saturday. On Tuesday he played chess in a chess club formed by his grandfather. All day Thursday was free, but two Thursday evenings each month were taken up with his astronomy class meeting. Danny was eight when he started attending *Language Wise* training. His parents pushed him hard for a reason. There were complications at birth and they were told that he was developmentally delayed and that his I.Q. might never reach the normal range. "I just refused to accept it," Danny's mom explained. "I'm glad I did. Look at him now." At five Danny's I.Q. was 104. At eight it was 116. We've stayed in touch with Danny and his fam-ily. He's ten now and has discontinued Spanish lessons, but has filled that time with private art lessons.

DANNY'S STEADY CLIMB

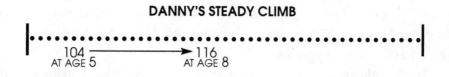

Another important piece of information comes to us from research con-ducted by Kegan and Freeman. In this study researchers found that children who experienced the greatest I.Q. loss from four and a half to six years of age were those who demonstrated the greatest dependency on their parents. One might derive from these findings that children perform best when they're confi-dent and independent. This study also revealed that the greatest gains from six to ten years of age were experienced by those with a high achievement drive or reported high competitiveness. Although we'll explore the mechanisms behind the achievement drive in more detail in the next chapter, let's have a brief look at a few important studies before we move on.

A 1983 study conducted by McClelland and Pilon backs up the link between achievement drive and performance. These researchers conducted achievement tests on thirty-one year old adults whose mothers had been extensively inter-viewed twenty-five years earlier by Sears, Maccoby and Lewin (1957) regarding their child rearing practices. This study reveals that the highest correlate to achievement drive is clearly the mother's belief that it is very important for her child to perform well in school. This was true across all socio-economic strata, with the highest effect among the children of white collar workers.

"The Reward of a Thing Well Done is Having Done It."
What is the Reward of a Thing Done Badly?

This study brings to bear the place of competition and achievement in the daily course of instruction. But many educators and parents feel uncomfortable encouraging children to out-achieve their peers. There has been a growing trend in the last two decades to encourage knowledge for knowledge's sake, rather than for the sake of an edge on one's classmate. Certainly we do not want to make our children into little gladiators, battling it out at the spelling bee or in the one minute multiplication tables. And we certainly want children to appreciate the sense of accomplishment that accompanies proficiency. However, it is reasonable to want a child to be the best he can be, and he shouldn't have to apologize or perform less well if his best is better than the child with whom he shares his lunch. Ultimately parents and educators must ask themselves the question—if, as Victor Hugo says, "The reward of a thing well done is having done it," what is the reward of a thing poorly done?

One solution to this dilemma may be to encourage children to focus on doing better than they did the last time they performed a task. "Last week you spelled four words correctly on the spelling bee. This week you spelled all but one correctly. Good job!!" This focus is more positive than trying to beat your friends, and in the long haul may prove more productive, as it keeps the focus on the child's own performance, over which he has some degree of control, as opposed to the group's performance, over which he has very little control. Since 1969 motivation psychologists have realized that motivation is not as simple as early theorists imagined. A 1969 motivation study (Verof) indicates that what we think of as achievement may in fact be two things—one intrinsic and one extrinsic. Verof found that children as young as two and a half display pleasure at improving their skills over their own previous performance. The fact that enjoyment of one's own progress appears so early is an indication that intrinsic achievement may be a natural development, an inherent part of human nature. It isn't until much later, between kindergarten and sixth grade, that children learn to compare their own performance with the performance of others—extrinsic achievement.

This theme is supported by other research indicating that subjects scoring high on achievement tests have more awareness and concern for their own performance than they do for the performance of others. They are also more likely to be able to give accurate observations about their own performance as opposed to the performance of others in the group. These high achievement subjects seem fully focused on their own efforts, not the efforts of their peers.

"They Can Because They Think They Can." *Or Do They Think They Can Because They Can?*

Do children high in achievement motive do better because they set and undertake higher goals for themselves? According to numerous studies, they do not. In fact, subjects scoring high on achievement motivation choose tasks of moderate difficulty where their chance of success is fairly high, while their low achievement classmates are five times as likely to choose tasks that are too difficult or too easy for them. This may offer valuable insight into the success of those high in achievement. In a 1980 study Weiner suggests that students with a high achievement motive may well choose moderately difficult tasks in order to allow themselves feedback on their performance. It may be that children high in achievement perform better because they use their own performance as a gauge for their next attempt, thereby staying in touch with their own capability, and learning from each attempt, each failure and success. This idea has been tested by many motivation researchers.

In a 1982 study researchers Raynor and Entin told subjects what their success rate expectations were when asked to solve sixty anagrams. Some subjects were told they were expected to solve six correctly, some were told thirty, and some were told fifty-four. Later the subjects were tested for their achievement drive. The high achievement drive subjects tended to have performed better when told they were expected to solve thirty items, a moderately difficult task compared to six or fifty-four, which would be too easy or too hard. The low achievement subjects showed no such tendency.

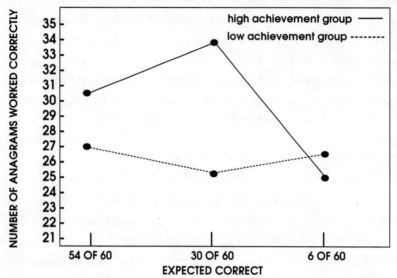

EFFECTS OF HIGH AND LOW ACHIEVEMENT DRIVE ON PERFORMANCE

Making My Child Smarter Seems Easy

It would seem, based on all this, that the formula for success is to give birth to a child with reasonably good brain genes, encourage him to be independent, send him to a good school, enroll him in piano lessons, join a chess club, subscribe to *Crossword Quarterly*, encourage him to do well (consistently), mix often and voila—a brain surgeon will emerge, or at least a podiatrist. Well maybe—but what if you can't afford a good school or can't find one within a six day drive? What if the only piano teacher within a two hundred mile radius has a seven year waiting list, or your child absolutely hates piano lessons? What if he consistently uses the pages of *Crossword Quarterly* to make paper airplanes, or those tiny little paper footballs the kids like to shoot around the room? What if you consistently encourage him—even demand that he do well—and he consistently brings home grades of C+? What if his idea of achievement is having the latest Tommy Hilfiger tennis shoes, retailing for $129.99? Many well intentioned parents are stunned to learn that junior won't play along at this super kid game. It would seem easier to get the family cat into architectural college than to get junior in.

Kids like these are among the ranks of those achieving well below expectation, in school, and in life. According to an international report, *Literacy Skills for the Knowledge Society* (Human Resources Development Canada), the United States scores second to lowest (above Poland) among thirteen countries, in prose, document, and computational literacy. This painfully low number is a sad showing considering that in the U.S. your child has a one in four chance of graduating from college. Architectural or medical school seems a high expectation indeed given that this study revealed that only 45% of Americans with a high school diploma will actually read a book this week.

In another study, *National Adult Literacy* (1992), only 5% of adult Americans reached prose and document literacy level five of five. Only 17% reached level four of five, and only 32% reached level three. This means that only half of America's adults have achieved only basic literacy skills—skills as basic as entering requested information in the appropriate place on a form, and being able to sift out information irrelevant to the text.

So What's a Parent to Do?

We know that we can affect intelligence scores by as much as fifty points from age six to eighteen. And we know that fifty percent of intelligence is language related. So we know we can make our children more *language wise*. The next question is how. If you're like me, you have precious little time to donate to this super kid thing. Junior had better pay attention and get the main idea fast, before the next promotion, business trip, birth of a sibling, move to another state, health challenge, divorce, return to graduate school, change of occupation, etc, etc, etc... In short, American parents have very little time to pay to their aspiring geniuses, so whatever they do needs to work the first time. That's where *Language Wise* comes in. *Language Wise* is designed to improve the vocabulary, comprehension, logical reasoning, creativity, composition, and exposition of children age six*ish* to twenty. The theoretical basis should be applied by the time the child is four*ish*, and ideally from birth. This program was developed at Read America, the developers of the internationally recognized reading method Phono-Graphix. *Language Wise* has been field tested by 237 parents, teachers and clinicians who've reported gains in vocabulary, reasoning, writing, grammar, creativity, comprehension, ability to work independently, and attitude toward language related activities. The following reveals the responses to survey questions asked of these teachers.

I am using the lessons: (109) as a teacher   (82) as a parent   (46) in a clinic

I work with some students with learning disabilities (91).

I do not work with learning disabled students (146).

Age of children whose parents used the book with them (5-13).

Age range of students using the book with teachers   (7-17).

My child/students responded to lessons within:

   32% said 1 month

   43% said 2 months

   17% said 3 months

   8% said 4 months

I observed or measured gains in these areas:

   92% vocabulary gains

   84% improved reasoning

   94% improved writing

   94% improved comprehension

   81% increase in creativity

   96% improved attitude toward language activities

   81% improved grammar

   83% increased ability to work independently

I would recommend this book to parents 97%.

I would recommend this book to teachers 96%.

In addition to this survey we pre and post tested fifty-seven students age eight to eighteen on the Peabody Individual Achievement Test (PIATr) to test their comprehension and on the Peabody Picture Vocabulary Test (PPVTr) to test their vocabulary. The average time of *Language Wise* instruction was twenty-one hours. The average comprehension gain was eighteen months and the average vocabulary gain was eleven months.

Best of all, *Language Wise* is quick. With all the focus on quality time, we're happy to report that it's also fun. Many parents have learned the value of spending time talking with their children, rather than watching yet another sitcom. *Language Wise* offers a self-contained plan for enhancing your child's verbal intelligence. The activities are easy to follow, and can be done while engaging in other activities. One parent told us that our *Connections* game was known at their house as *the car game*. Another family reported that they play many of the games during their Tuesday night bowling league. "We get the whole team going." Another family reports that, "Now we have something to talk about at dinner other than the neighbors." If you're a classroom teacher, you'll find *Language Wise* easy to implement into your daily schedule. The theoretical basis can add power to any curriculum. The lessons can be folded into any instructional plan. Use the lessons as a morning warm-up, waiting for the children on the board like a familiar friend, as a transition activity, or on rainy days. One retired teacher who works now as a substitute part time in an inner city elementary school wrote this on her *Language Wise* survey, "I wouldn't go in without it. When the kids realize they've got me for the day they say, *'Oh we're not doing any work, we're doing those games!'* Little do they know." *Language Wise* offers you more than just an educational edge—it offers you a shared activity that's fun!

How Do I Get Started?

If you're working with a young child of five to seven, you've got plenty of time. The best plan is to start early and use the activities twice a week for a while, working your way up to three times a week. If you're working with an older child or young adult, we recommend more frequent exposure to the lessons. Three to four times per week is a good plan. As we've mentioned, these activities can be done while doing other activities, but we do recommend one sit-down, serious lesson per week. It's best to read the entire book before getting started. That way you'll have a good overview of the entire program. Once you've got a global understanding of the plan, jump in and do it. There is no particular order of presentation, though some lessons warn that they should follow others. For the most part you can skip around and pick and choose. We do recommend that all the lessons be used at some time. At Read America, we do one or two lessons per sitting. If the child is a successful reader we mix supervised lessons with independent assignments. If the child is not the best speller, we recommend that he be allowed to do independent writing activities without getting bogged down in perfect spelling. These can be edited at the next supervised lesson. We also mix *Language Wise* instruction with Phono-Graphix instruction for children with reading or spelling delays. Parents can use the book *Reading Reflex—The Foolproof Phono-Graphix Method* at home with their children.

 How to Increase Your Child's Verbal Intelligence doesn't just give you lessons to do with your child, it gives you the rationale behind the lessons, building a strong case for the use of the lessons by instructing the reader in the nature of verbal intelligence, its components and how they relate to one another and to the child's performance in school and in life. In chapter two of *How to Increase Your Child's Verbal Intelligence* the reader will discover the secrets behind the learning drive, what moves the learner, and how this mechanism can fail. Chapter three explores the nature of language as a reflection of the physical universe, with a look at the place of vocabulary and grammar in the larger picture of emerging verbal intelligence. Chapter four looks at the acquisition of language from birth through school, giving the reader clear goals and milestones, and an understanding of the forces driving the acquisition of verbal intelligence. Chapter five focuses on the role of attention and memory in the development of verbal intelligence, how these interrelate and how they relate to other aspects of verbal intelligence and learning. This chapter also explores the difference between kinds of memory, leaving parents and teachers better prepared to improve this critical component of verbal intelligence. Chapter six investigates the parts of logical reasoning and creativity that relate to the development of verbal intelligence, exploring the origins of creativity and illustrating ways to integrate creative and analytic reasoning into all aspects of problem solving. Section two of *How to Increase Your Child's Verbal Intelligence* contains the lessons that are built upon all of this and that make up the highly successful *Language Wise* verbal intelligence course. At the front of section two is a chart listing typical reading and writing activities expected of children as they pass through school. Under each activity are listed the *Language Wise* lessons that relate to that activity. We suggest that after you've read the chapters and come to a global understanding of verbal intelligence you move swiftly on to begin exploring the lessons with your child. It's important to understand that this book is not just a course for your child, but a course for you as well. If you think of the lessons in the back as your child's work and the chapters in the front as your work, you'll be better prepared to meet the challenges that raising a verbally intelligent child will present. Not all of the benefits of what you learn from the chapters will be applied when you use the lessons with your child. Much of what you learn will equip you with the crucial understanding to help him in his day to day development as he makes the journey toward adulthood. These benefits will not end when your child reaches a certain age, and they may not end with your child. In pilot testing many parents and teachers report increased interest in their interactions with spouses, coworkers, employees and employers. One principal of a large urban school reported, "It's a course in how people learn, develop, and communicate. *Language Wise* will help you with all the children in your life, even the grown up ones."

CHAPTER TWO

THE LEARNING CURVE

HUMAN MOTIVATION

In this chapter you will learn

What learning is and how parents and educators can be fooled. How to tell real from temporary learning.

The tricks nature plays on learners and how parents can put these tricks to work for their children.

What kind of feedback parents and teachers should be offering to their children and students. How to turn errors into learning.

The difference between a natural incentive and an extrinsic motivator.

How individual differences impact learning.

How parenting styles affect the development of individual differences.

A parent survey to help you channel the quality of instructional time spent with your child.

Every parent and teacher wants the best possible education for his or her child or students. But what does that actually mean in instructional terms? As part of our standard intake forms and our teacher training course, we surveyed two hundred seventeen parents and teachers at the Read America clinic from 1995 to 1997 with the intention of discovering their feelings about what was important in their children's educational experience. We're asking that you complete this brief survey before you get started with the rest of the chapter.

Please rank in order of importance your five highest goals for your child's education.

1. _____

2. _____

3. _____

4. _____

5. _____

Answer "mostly agree" or "mostly disagree" to the following statements:

	mostly agree	mostly disagree
Children learn in different ways.	❏	❏
Teachers and parents should be prepared to try different approaches to teaching two children the same skill.	❏	❏
Instructional activities should be fun and entertaining.	❏	❏
Children shouldn't be asked to do anything until they have had enough instruction that they can succeed at it.	❏	❏

When asked to "Please rank in order of importance your five highest goals for your child's/students' educational experience," the most frequently chosen first goal indicated was, "my child/students remains safe at school." The most frequently chosen second goal was, "my child/students enjoys school." Are these reasonable goals for our children's education? Of course our children's safety and happiness are important, but should they be at the top of a list of *educational goals*?

The most frequently chosen third goal was that "my child/students feels good about his/her/their performance at school." This answer was chosen by more parents and teachers than "my child/students performs well at school." Do these parents and teachers place a higher emphasis on the perception of learning than they do on learning itself? If you answered "mostly agree" to these questions your answers are in keeping with eighty-four percent of the two hundred seventeen teachers and parents we've asked these questions. And you, like they, though your heart may be in the right place, are wrong. If parents and teachers are to get the most out of instructional time with children, we need to understand how and why children learn.

What is Learning?

Learning is defined as *a permanent change in behavior*. Much of what goes on at home and at school that appears on the surface to be learned is really only a *temporary* change in behavior, with no real learning taking place. There is much about how children learn that the average parent and even the average teacher doesn't know that may be affecting whether his or her children and students are making permanent or just temporary changes in behavior—whether real learning is occurring or just an illusion of learning. This information is locked in research journals and university textbooks on the topics of 'learning theory' and 'motivation'. Unfortunately most of this never makes its way to teacher training programs or to parenting classes. In this chapter we'll explore some of the classic research in these fields and attempt to illustrate a basic model of the learning process so that readers can make serious critical judgments about whether their children and students are learning and make necessary changes in routine and format when they're not.

The Driving Force Behind Learning

There is a driving force that sometimes gently and sometimes not so gently guides us all toward intellectual growth. This is a common force within all humans. It's the innate tendency to create and maintain a harmonious relationship between the self and the environment. Darwin called it *survival of the fittest*, Connon referred to it as *homeostasis*, Freud called it *hedonism*, and his follower Maslow popularized the term *self-actualization*. Motivation researchers Miller and Dollard called it the *anxiety reduction model*. Writers of prose have referred often to the *greener grass across the meadow*. Developmental psychologist Jean Piaget coined the term *equilibration* to describe this naturally occurring phenomenon, and said, "It is the innate tendency to organize one's experiences so as to assure maximal adaptation to the environment." In very simple terms the phenomenon is man looking for a better fit between himself and the world.

We'll have a look at how this mechanism works through the experiences of a five year old. Sally is a pretty typical five year old. She attends kindergarten at a large public school in New York City. She likes ice cream and birthday parties and new dresses and playing box ball with her older brother Jake. She can count to fourteen and then gets a bit confused beyond that number. She knows her address and her telephone number, which was a big help shortly before Christmas when she got separated from her mother while shopping in Macy's. The nice police officer who found her was able to take her right home. Sally didn't even cry. When she was reunited with her mother she said, "It's OK. I was just looking for you." In February Sally and her mother went to stay at Auntie Grace's house in Atlanta to help Auntie Grace take care of her new baby son. On their second night at Auntie Grace's house Sally's mommy asked Sally if she'd like to call home to talk to Daddy and Jake. Sally missed the rest of her family and said yes she would like very much to do that. She dialed her phone number and a strange lady's voice told her, "Your call can not be completed as you've dialed it." She tried to tell the voice that it was her phone number and that her Daddy was home and he should answer, but the voice didn't pay any attention and only repeated the same message. When Sally went to tell Mommy about the lady's voice on the phone, Mommy told her that she needed to dial the area code. Sally asked what that was and Mommy told her it was a bigger number that she needed to use when they were not so near to their house. Sally liked making calls, it made her feel like a big girl, so Mommy wrote down a one, and then three other numbers on a piece of paper on Auntie Grace's telephone table and told Sally to press these numbers first and then the phone number. Sally did this and was very happy to talk to Daddy. Daddy asked her if she was having fun at Auntie Grace's house. She said she was. He asked if she had learned anything new since he had seen her. She said she had learned about the special numbers you have to dial when you're far away. Sally called Daddy every other night for the whole month that she and Mommy stayed in Atlanta. By the beginning of the second week she didn't even need to look at the piece of paper with the numbers on it. She already knew what they were. After Sally and Mommy were home in New York for about a week, Mommy said they should call Auntie Grace and check on her and the baby. Sally liked making phone calls so she climbed up on the kitchen counter next to the phone. Mommy opened her blue flowered phone directory to Auntie Grace's number and showed Sally where it was on the page. Sally dialed the numbers and after a few rings Uncle Bill answered. "Hi Uncle Bill. Your area code is 404," she announced. "Well so it is!" Uncle Bill's deep voice responded. "You sure are a smarty aren't you. I hope little Billy turns out to be as smart as his cousin Sally is." Sally felt proud and giggled.

The process through which Sally progressed illustrates the innate tendency for equilibration. Sally, who perceived herself as an adept user of telephones, discovered she wasn't the expert she thought. This put her into a state of disequilibrium. So she took the appropriate steps toward gaining proficiency to the next level—mastering the area code, and re-establishing equilibrium (expert status). An important element in this process is that old information is the basis for new. Had Sally not already become adept at local calls, she would not have been in a position to become adept at toll calls. In this way, the learner is able to catapult off existing skills and information into new skills and information. Later these new skills and information become old skills and information, placing the learner in a position to try new stunts and thereby take in additional new skills and information. On and on it goes, the old laying down the turf for the new. So long as the world holds new challenges, old limits must be broken to meet them. For the reader who likes models, a model of this innate tendency might look something like the figure to the right.

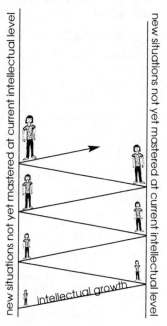

The Learning Dilemma

There are some necessary components to the model we've illustrated. For this intricate innate process to unfold, the learner must be allowed to encounter new experiences, and he must be allowed to fail at them. These are fighting words to some parents and teachers. Looking back at our survey at the beginning of this chapter, we see that parents and teachers on the whole don't like the notion of their children and students failing. However, without failure, there is no disequilibrium, no limit, no *reason* to take in new information—no *motivation*.

Motivation psychologists Miller and Dollard coined the term *learning dilemma* to discuss this phenomenon. They summarized that old skills and information must be activated in order to solve problems in the environment. When a problem could not be solved with the old information and skills, failure would occur and anxiety would result. New skills and information would be taken into the learner's repertoire in order to solve the problems relieving the anxiety—and learning would occur. The dilemma—learning always follows failure. Is this apparently critical failure component present in the lives of our children? According to the answers to the survey that opens this chapter, sufficient opportunities to *fail* and thereby *learn* may be missing from the lives of some children, with caring parents and teachers carefully removing the opportunities for failure from the paths of their learners. Yet as parents and teachers our success at handling the *learning dilemma* is largely dependent upon our willingness to let children fail. An important prerequisite to this for most teachers and parents would be understanding how that failure links up eventually to new learning which the child will view ultimately as a success.

The End Justifies the Means

Our years of training teachers and observing teachers in classrooms has led us to believe that most teachers think that teaching is removing instructional obstacles. To the contrary, it's placing appropriate challenges and in the right order that is the basis of good teaching. But this is only one aspect of the teaching process. Another aspect is in assuring that new information is available following the failure, so that learning can take place. This new information can come as direct feedback from the error, as in self-correcting materials, or it can come from the teacher, as in direct instruction. This critically important structure is the backbone of *Language Wise*. This is the formula that this book will carefully guide you toward. The diagram on the next page explores this mechanism.

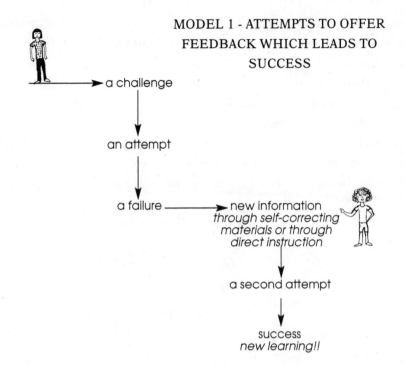

MODEL 1 - ATTEMPTS TO OFFER
FEEDBACK WHICH LEADS TO
SUCCESS

a challenge

an attempt

a failure ────────► new information
*through self-correcting
materials or through
direct instruction*

a second attempt

success
new learning!!

As long as the new information is there following failure, the failure becomes something of a reward, offering the new information that leads to the eventual success. Numerous studies (Deci, 1975; Birch, Marlin & Rotter, 1984; Lepper & Greene, 1975, 1978) indicate that feedback may be the only valid reward, and that prizes and incentives that teachers and parents tend to think of as rewards are actually demotivating. In study after study, children have been found to discontinue a task when a reward was offered. The child who is offered feedback about her performance as an incentive learns early that errors are a means to a successful end. In this way, teachers who dislike seeing children fail can understand that the end justifies the means. The alternatives to this are not good. The following is a learning model in which the teacher or parent provides only experiences at which the learner can succeed. Whenever new information is added the child is only allowed to practice it after the teacher is certain she will succeed.

MODEL 2 - NO LEARNING

practice   *practice*   *practice*   *practice*

boring boring boring boring boring boring

The teacher can be fooled into thinking learning is occurring in this model because there is no failure—when in fact without the chance of failure, there is no chance of learning.

In the following model the child is allowed to try and fail over and over again. This model is becoming more and more prevalent in our schools as the notion of learning disabilities takes over. This notion places the blame always on the child. *If Sally didn't learn, it's because Sally can't learn.* The instructional process and methodologies are never examined, never considered as the possible problem. In time, the child learns that failure is okay.

MODEL 3 - FAILURE IS EASY

In a 1968 study (deCharms & Carpenter) researchers found that low achieving students are likely to attempt things that are much too difficult for a good chance of success. These low achievers seem happy to fail repeatedly, placing value on the lofty attempt rather than eventual success. Seligman popularized the term *learned helplessness* to describe the effect of being faced over and over again with a challenge over which one has no control. As mentioned in chapter one, Weiner (1980) hypothesized that high achievers succeed where low achievers fail because high achievers use their failed attempts at moderately difficult tasks as a diagnostic tool for making subsequent attempts. This supports the efficacy of model number one where the reward is in the feedback gained from the error. Additionally it may explain some of the variance in verbal intelligence, and why some children are happy to fail again and again as in model number three, happy to settle for having tried a very difficult task.

To Err is Human (and Instructional)

In building verbal intelligence, it can be said that the better the instruction, the more failures (rewards) occur on the way to the success. Some information and skills are so intricate that it's best to isolate and deal with just one error at a time. When teaching very intricate skills and information, it's generally best to deal with each error or issue in isolation. In such cases, the model ends up looking like a chain of attempts, failures and subsequent attempts. The important thing to remember is that each failure acts as a reward by providing new information and opportunities to try new skills. When a task is well done, the child learns that all efforts contain a reward in the lessons learned. The best possible outcome is the child who takes this logic so far as to realize that even with very little new information there is a lesson in the knowledge that the attempt made was not the correct one. So, process of elimination is a rewarding experience and an instructional one in the absence of all other instruction.

Researchers in the 1970s (deCharms & Muir; Perlmutter, Scharff, Karsh & Monty) examined the effects of children seeing a goal as an attainable challenge rather than an unattainable threat. They found that this is the highest correlator to eventual success at tasks attempted. They found that these children choose moderately difficult tasks, use their own failed attempts to gain feedback for the next attempt, have a clear understanding of controllable versus non-controllable outcomes, prefer activities they choose over assigned activities, and that they prefer to be in control of the scheduling and flow of activities. These children were termed 'origins' by the researchers conducting these studies. Psychologists consider the characteristics seen in the 1970s 'origins' studies to be *traits*. Chanowitz and Langer (1982) conducted similar studies, concluding that the subjects with the highest performance were those with the highest *self-efficacy*. Albert Bandura (1982) also commented on performance of high achievers, saying that they demonstrated a sense of personal responsibility about their tasks.

Development of the M Factor
Natural Incentives, Emotions, and Motives

There are of course other factors playing into the learning process. In Sally's case, had she been a less curious child or had she received less encouragement from her parents she might not have learned to use the phone even for local calls by age five, and when thwarted by a missing area code, she might have given up—set the task aside for some more accomplished user of phones to undertake.

Although the driving force behind learning is innate and fixed by the nature of the human beast, there is much that is dependent upon the particular environment of the learner—how rich or poor it is in natural incentives. In Sally's case, the environment includes eager and proud family members. Mom was happy to offer Sally a lesson in area codes. Dad was delighted to hear from Sally. Uncle Bill offered Sally praise for her accomplishments. The attention that Sally received for her actions fulfilled her desire for contact. Contact is one of the natural incentives isolated by motivation psychologists. Natural incentives play an important part in the learning process. How willing we are to approach or avoid new information is guided by our natural incentives and how they direct our emotions and motives. Other natural incentives are *impact* on the environment and *variety*. Specific emotions have been found to be associated with natural incentives. Below is a chart showing three motives, the emotions that fuel them, and the natural incentives that drive the emotions (Eckman, 1971).

NATURAL INCENTIVES, THEIR RELATED EMOTIONS AND RESULTING MOTIVES

NATURAL INCENTIVE	EMOTION	MOTIVE
variety	interest/surprise	achievement
impact	anger/excitement	power
contact	joy/happiness/pleasure	affiliation

The relationship between natural incentives, emotions and motivation is an intricate one. Let's define each of these terms and discuss their relationship to one another. *Natural incentives* are naturally occurring stimuli in the world around us that have been found to have a strong effect on emotions as listed on the chart above. Motivation psychologists call this effect an *incentive value*. *Emotions* occur in response to naturally occurring incentives. Emotions amplify motives, accompanying them and adding fuel to their effect on behavior. In this sense, they supply the energy to maintain the motivation. It is the *motives* that actually drive behavior. The affiliation motive, for instance, will drive a five year old off the swing set and on a search for his mother because previous contact with her has brought him pleasure. In time affiliation will be a motivation acting on his behavior in new experiences.

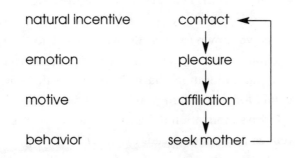

A seven year old will be drawn to the science center in her classroom because her natural incentive to variety is stimulated while watching the ants in the ant farm burrow tunnels through the chunky wet sand.

Based on this interplay between naturally occurring incentives, emotions and motivation, it would seem that if we want our children to be motivated—to achieve, to be affiliative with others, to have impact on the world around them—we should allow them lots of opportunities to experience naturally occurring incentives, help them to understand their emotions and to realize the relationship between the incentive and the emotion. Much of this occurs on the playing field so to speak. Johnny sees a large horse perform dressage and looks interested. "Oh Johnny, I see you're excited. It must be that the horse has caught your interest. Let's go have a closer look and talk to the man. Maybe we can learn what it's all about!" Sometimes emotions that appear to be negative play out to the learner's advantage. Here's a real-life clip from a conversation I overheard in a playground not too long ago. This teacher helped the child realize how he was feeling and why. And she showed him a way to successfully act on his feelings. Four year old Jason was working with five year old George to build a sand castle in the school sand box. A fight broke out. The teacher intervened. "I can tell you're very angry with George. Is that because he won't let you build the sand castle the way you want to build it? I can see from how upset you are that you really want to do this your way, so maybe you and George should play away from each other. You can build your own sand castle over here. And George can build his over there." By helping children to see the relationship between incentives and their emotions, we put children in charge of their emotions and help them learn to use them as fuel for motivation. The alternative in the above vignette would have been for Jason's motivation to be squashed by the frustration he felt at George taking over his project. Instead, the teacher managed the situation beautifully and Jason's lesson was—*"I'm not really angry with George, I just want to do this myself—and that's okay."*

Should I Offer My Child Incentives to Improve His Performance?

It's important to draw a clear distinction between natural and external rewards. Offering a child a sticker or a quarter is not the same thing as offering him a hug or a thumbs up. The use of incentives has become common practice in education and child rearing, with an entire industry growing out of the phenomenon. Considerable research has been done on this topic offering strong evidence that rewards and incentives are not necessarily the best way to motivate your child.

A 1975 study (Deci) found that children engaged in a self-selected learning task discontinued the task prior to completion when a performance reward was offered by researchers. In an earlier study (Cuvo, 1974), rewards were offered to children age ten, thirteen and eighteen as an incentive to recall lists of words. The subjects were told that increased rehearsal of the word list would result in greater incentives. Ten year olds showed no increase in rehearsal, while the thirteen and eighteen year olds did have a moderate increase. No group showed improvement in overall memory from the increased practice. Despite the age of these studies and the fact that they have stood the test of time, they still appear in contemporary motivation textbooks as the accepted model, yet the walls of classrooms and refrigerator doors around the country are lined with the paraphernalia of reward systems.

Perhaps one reason external motivators are largely ineffective at motivating or improving performance is that they are dependent upon the judgment of another. According to Albert Bandura, developer of *social learning theory*, "People do not behave just to suit the preferences of others. Much of their behavior is motivated and regulated through internal standards and self-evaluative reactions to their own actions" (*Cognition and Psychotherapy*, 1985). According to Bandura, behavior is largely self-regulated through internal standards and *self*-incentives. According to Bandura there are four processes at work in this self-regulatory system.

comparisons of perceived performance to internal standards
performance of others in the same activity
valuation of the activity
personal appraisal of the situational factors affecting performance

Bandura explains that activation of this self-evaluative system requires both personal standards and knowledge of the level of one's own performance. Without these the system fails.

Given this, it would seem that instead of offering children a sticker for a job well done, teachers and parents should be offering them solid but attainable standards and a means of evaluating their own performance against those standards.

Individual Differences and Traits

As we've said, equilibration is a fixed structure that all humans share. And we've said that all humans are affected by naturally occurring incentives in the world around them. We've also said that natural incentives bring out emotions which we all experience at various times in life. On the surface, humans sound pretty predictable. Yet, we're not. We're not all the same. There are elements of humanness that are unique and guide us gently in different directions and at different speeds. Three men may behave very differently in the same situation because of the traits that guide their behavior. *Traits* appear at a fairly early age and tend to last throughout the lifespan. They affect how we manage and direct our motives, which ultimately affects the success of our behavior. It can be said that our traits are the baggage we bring to our behavior. In many cases the baggage is a set of helpful tools. In some cases it's a burden. Psychologists define traits as *any relatively enduring way in which one individual differs from another*. So where learning and motivation theorists have studied what is consistent among people, personality and trait theorists have studied what is different and unique. While the study of learning theory will help us see consistencies across people, the study of traits will help us see consistency within the individual. Let's look on the next page at some of the traits studied by personality researcher Raymond Cattell

(1965) to see how they play into equilibration and motivation to ultimately affect performance. Traits are measured in degrees from the left column to the right. In Cattell's personality profile, each trait is given a score of one to ten from left to right.

Personality Traits

reserved									outgoing
less intelligent									more intelligent
affected by feelings									emotionally stable
submissive									dominant
serious									happy-go-lucky
expedient									conscientious
timid									venturesome
tough-minded									sensitive
trusting									suspicious
practical									imaginative
forthright									shrewd
self-assured									apprehensive
1	2	3	4	5	6	7	8	9	10

Reflecting back on Sally, the phone expert at the age of five, peruse the traits above and see if you can isolate some that Sally probably possesses, based on what you currently know about her. Don't overextend your assumptions. Pick a few that seem obvious. Our analysis appears below.

Sally's Personality Traits

reserved									outgoing ✓
less intelligent									more intelligent ✓
affected by feelings									emotionally stable
submissive									dominant
✓ serious									happy-go-lucky
expedient									conscientious
timid									venturesome ✓
tough-minded									sensitive
trusting									suspicious
practical									imaginative
forthright									shrewd
✓ self-assured									apprehensive
1	2	3	4	5	6	7	8	9	10

Clearly Sally may have other characteristics, but these are the ones we've seen demonstrated based on her story so far. With these traits as tools, our model of Sally's behavior might look something like this.

Being aware of Sally's unique traits allows her parents and teachers to make educated decisions about what experiences to put before Sally, and it offers important information about when to offer assistance and how much or how little assistance to offer. In this way the informed or sensitive parent or teacher is better able to match the needs of the child. We've talked about how Sally's traits played into her behavior in making phone calls. A look at the chart below shows how those traits might have actually driven Sally's mother's behavior in helping Sally to succeed.

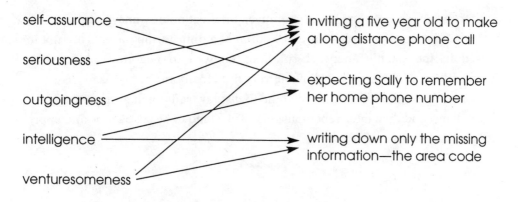

Needless to say this process becomes cyclical, with Sally's mom's behavior toward Sally reinforcing Sally's traits.

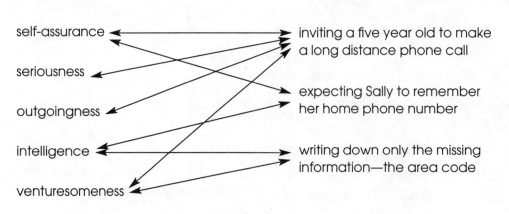

Parenting Syles and the Development of Individual Differences and Motives

A 1981 study (Lewis) revealed that parenting styles and the development of individual traits of children is a two way street, with particular traits correlating with particular parental styles. Lewis' research was based on previous research into parenting styles conducted by Diana Baumrind (1971, 1979). Through extensive observation and questionnaires, Baumrind isolated three distinct parenting styles.

Authoritarian Parents

Authoritarian parents are firm, punitive, unaffectionate, unsympathetic, detached and sparing in their praise. Children of authoritarian parents are not involved in the establishment of rules, or allowed to negotiate about rules. Independence is thwarted by allowing very little freedom.

Lewis found that these children tend to display traits such as aggressiveness, dependency and then later rebelliousness. They tend to be suspicious and apprehensive in their interactions.

Permissive Parents

Permissive parents do not exert control over their children. Children have very few responsibilities. They tend to be treated like adults. These children are allowed to set and alter their own schedules at will.

Children of permissive parents tend to develop traits such as impulsiveness, sexual promiscuity, selfishness and aggression.

Authoritative Parents

Authoritative parents see the relationship between parents and children as reciprocal and complementary. They give equal portions of rights and responsibilities.   Parents reason with their children, allowing negotiations that are reasonable, and listen to objections of their children. There are very few conflicts in these homes. Parents are firm, loving and understanding. Their demands are reasonable, rational and consistent. They set limits that allow for independence. Children have a clear understanding of what's expected of them and what they can expect of their parents.

Children whose parents are authoritative tend to be friendly, cooperative, competent, self-reliant, independent, happy, socially responsible and, central to our topic, *intellectually assertive.*

My Child Can be so Negative—Doesn't This Get in the Way of Learning?

As children mature and develop, another factor begins to take shape and affect how they process intellectual information. *Explanatory style* can be defined as *how pessimistic or optimistic the child is in viewing and processing the events of his life.* Numerous studies have indicated that children with a pessimistic explanatory style are more likely to show symptoms of depression (Hops, Lewisohn, Andrews & Roberts, 1990), and have an overall lower mastery orientation (Altman & Gotlib, 1988; Hops et al., 1990). A pessimistic explanatory style appears to spring from early experiences over which the child has little or no control. A positive explanatory style appears to evolve in children who have had many early experiences with a high degree of individual control over the outcome.

My Child is so Moody—How Does This Affect How She Learns?

Moods and moodiness are more transient than explanatory style. Where an explanatory style is consistent and predictable, moods are often brought on by external events. Bower (1981) instigated a study to discover the effect of moods on learning. Subjects in a good mood tended to recall more positive information, while subjects in a bad mood tended to remember more negative information. Bower termed this phenomenon a *mood congruency effect*. The ability of the parent or teacher to influence mood in learning situations was demonstrated by Perrig (1988) when the Bower experiment was recreated. In Perrig's version of the study the subject's mood was not established, but rather the subject was told to "behave as if you're in a good/bad mood." The results were the same in this mood setting study as they were in the original Bower study.

In a Perfect World

It would seem from all of this that the best way to raise and educate an intelligent, motivated, high achieving, happy child would be to offer lots of encouragement, praise and opportunities for freedom with responsibility. Create an environment rich in natural incentives, offering lots of opportunity for self-selected tasks with internal or directed feedback—tasks in which success is measured against one's own past performance. And offer the child positive endings to challenging situations—endings that he can trace back to his own performance.

To the contrary it would seem that the worst environment would be one that has lots of parent or teacher selected tasks over which the learner has little or no impact or the impact is not perceivable to the learner, and success is measured against the group.

The survey on the following pages will help you adjust your instructional interactions with your child to the positive side of these two extremes.

PARENT SURVEY

Before you complete this book and begin using the *Language Wise* lessons as your child's verbal intelligence coach, please complete the following survey.

Language interaction section

1. *How many times per week do you and your child engage in a talk about an intangible concept?* ____ *never* ____ *1-2 times* ____*three or more times*

   *List some of the concepts*_____

   _____

   _____

   _____

2. *What percentage of your child's questions do you answer with another question?* ____ *less than 20%* ____ *20-50%* ____ *more than 50%*

   List two recent questions and your response _____

   _____

   _____

   _____

   _____

3. *Do you encourage your child to make judgments and then encourage him to tell you the basis of his judgment? List two examples.* · _____

   _____

   _____

   _____

   _____

4. *When your child doesn't know the meaning of a word, what do you do to teach him?* _____

   _____

   _____

5. *When your child is behaving badly do you ask him how he is feeling?* _____

   *When he describes a peer behaving badly do you ask him how he thinks the other child might be feeling?*_____

6. *Do you invite your child to describe things to you, and require lots of detail? If yes, offer an example.* _____

_____

_____

   Did you get the detail you expected? _____

7. *Do you create situations in which your child must problem-solve?* _____
   Offer two examples. _____

_____

_____

_____

_____

8. *Does your child remember things you've told him?* _____ *If not, how do you encourage him to begin to remember better?* _____

_____

_____

_____

_____

9. *Do you offer your child practice at comparison and contrast of things and concepts in his world? Offer two recent examples.* _____

_____

_____

_____

_____

_____

10. *Do you use analogies to teach your child? Give two recent examples.* _____

_____

_____

_____

_____

_____

11. When your child uses sloppy grammar, what do you do? _____

_____

_____

_____

_____

12. Do you offer your child experience at solving problems in which he must weigh multiple variables? Such as? _____

_____

_____

_____

_____

13. Do you allow your child to change his mind? Do you encourage him to vocalize his reasoning? _____

_____

_____

_____

_____

14. Does your child ever make a statement or write something that doesn't make sense? How do you handle it? Offer one example. _____

_____

_____

_____

15. Do you give your child opportunities to brainstorm? Offer two examples.

_____

_____

_____

16. Do you ever require inference of your child? How? _____

_____

_____

_____

17. *When your child deduces something, do you ask him how he knows that? Offer one recent example.* _____

_____

_____

_____

18. *How many books per week does your child read?* _____ *Do you feel that's enough?* _____

_____

19. *Do you ask specific questions about the books your child is reading?*

_____

_____

_____

_____

20. *How many times per week does your child do a writing activity?* _____ *Do you feel that's enough?* _____

_____

_____

Goals section

21. *What grades do you expect of your child?* ____ *As only* ____ *As and Bs* ____ *Bs* ____ *Bs and Cs* ____ *no less than a C* ____ *some Ds are okay*

22. *What is the consequence when your child does not meet this expectation?*

_____

_____

_____

_____

23. *How much education do you want your child to receive?*

____ *high school diploma* ____ *certification* ____ *two year degree*

____ *four year degree* ____ *graduate school*

CHAPTER THREE

IN A WORD
THE NATURE OF LANGUAGE

In this chapter you will learn

How language signs work.

How children learn language.

Why some children are more proficient at language than others.

What's wrong with traditional language instruction.

How to teach your child new vocabulary.

Sophie, the dog, obligingly drops her back end to the floor when I say that magical word, 'sit', and waits happily expecting a leash to be slipped over her furry head, for the commencement of the evening 'walkie'. When confronted with the same command, our fifteen year old assumes a challenging posture, narrows her eyes and asks, "Am I in trouble or something?" For both daughter and dog, 'sit' is a sign, a sign that stands for something, and has implications—walkies or trouble. Sophie's expectations were learned by repeated trials. For weeks I showed her the cookie jar, a clear plastic container with an ample supply of doggy treats, gave the 'sit' command, and then gave her the cookie. Eventually she learned that about half the time we carry out this exercise, the leash and much sought after walk follow. Although she would argue the point, Amanda learned her first few words in much the same way, but that is the topic of the next chapter. In this chapter, we will address the *nature* of language and save the *acquisition* of language for chapter three.

At my house, as at yours, 'sit' is a sign. It is one of the thousands of signs that we use and respond to each day. As I write this chapter other signs are reaching my senses. The faint smell of garlic frying tells me that the aforementioned Amanda has seen the written sign I left her in the designated place in the kitchen, and that she has begun preparing the evening meal. That quite pleasant sign is olfactory, reaching my brain by way of my nose. The sound of the Orlando dinner train whistle reminds me that it's already Friday, an auditory sign. Another auditory sign, a distant thunder clap, warns me of limited computer time before our evening thunderstorm moves in. A tiny flashing printer icon is alerting me to the fact that my printer is out of paper, a visual sign. And now Clifford the cat is meowing—his signal to alert me to the fact that despite her proximity to the cat food and the cat, Amanda has declined to feed him. I should have left her a sign about that too.

These are but a few examples of the signs that fill our lives. These signs are tools. Tools can be used for many purposes—for fixing your car, for writing a letter, for mashing potatoes. Signs are specific tools, used for making sense of your world. The smarter you are, the more signs you will be able to use, and the better sense you will make of your world. Some of the signs filling my world right now are invented and some are natural. Garlic does not smell when it's being cooked *so that* I'll know that dinner is forthcoming. But whistles *were* invented and put on trains *so that* people crossing tracks would get out of the way. Language is the second kind of sign. It is an invention of man. As we've pointed out in previous chapters correct use and understanding of oral language signs comprises fifty percent of intelligence scores. Without correct use of oral and written language signs your child will not be able to complete second and fourth grade standardized achievement tests, the PSAT in tenth grade, or the SAT in twelfth grade. In short, her entire educational career depends upon how good is her use of oral and written language. After leaving school her ability to fill out a job application and make small talk with the human resources coordinator who's interviewing her will be determined by her use of oral and written language signs. In school and in life the ability to use language effectively will determine her success or failure. Your ability to understand how language signs work and are learned will determine how successful you are at helping your child along the path to becoming *Language Wise*.

How Do Language Signs Work?

Early theoreticians and researchers thought that language might be a mental image. They postulated that words related to things and events would conjure up pictures of those things and events in the mind. This model of language has been discarded by contemporary linguists for several reasons.

> Although many people do make a lot of mental pictures when they speak and listen, they don't make pictures of everything. And many very intelligent people experience practically no mental images when they speak and process language (Gleason, 1989).

> Most words cannot be visually represented (Brown, 1968). Words like 'freedom', and 'clarity', 'serendipitous' and 'insidious'. In fact, the more sophisticated the word, the less likely you are of being able to pictorialize it with the full and specific credit it deserves.

> The grammatical structure of language makes mental pictures difficult and inefficient to use. For instance if I started off with, "The boy..." you might form an image of a contemporary male child of, say, five years. And then if I carried on with, "...sat translating the volume...," you might make him older. And then if I went on "...from its original Greek to the Latin of his countrymen," you would need to change his clothes and hair to the style appropriate to the Romans. This process is far too lengthy and cumbersome a model to yield the quality of mental functioning of most ten year olds.

And finally:

> Meaning isn't limited by a picture. Using our above example, let's imagine that you don't know much about the styles of the ancient Romans. That doesn't stop you from understanding the meaning of the sentence.

If Language isn't Mental Pictures, What is It?

According to MIT psycholinguist Steven Pinker, in his 1994 book *The Language Instinct* (p. 18),

> *"Language is a complex, specialized skill, which develops in the child spontaneously, without conscious effort or formal instruction..."*

American writer Ambrose Bierce called language

> *"The music with which we charm the serpents guarding another's treasure."*

Marshall McLuhan, director of the Center of Culture and Technology at the University of Toronto, described language as

"...man's richest art form, that which distinguishes him from the animal creation."

MIT linguist Noam Chomsky called language

"...that which associates sound and meaning in a particular way."

The father of cognitive developmental psychology, Jean Piaget, called language

"...the development of a symbolic and preconceptual thought."

These definitions, whether stylized prose or clinical in nature, reflect that although we know much about language, we do not know *exactly* what it is and how it works. Let's look at what we do know.

Most words are symbols or signs for things, concepts or events.

cat   dog

Other words allow us to modify or clarify those things, concepts or events.

frightened   big   brown

Other words represent actions of the things, concepts and events.

ran

Other words allow us to modify the actions.

away   quickly

And other words allow us to relate all of the above.

from   the   a

The frightened cat ran quickly away from a big brown dog.

We also know that the grammatical or syntactical structure of language acts as a formula that allows us some diversity in how we state a concept. So we could have said:

The big brown dog frightened a cat who ran quickly away.

or

The cat was frightened by a big brown dog and ran quickly away.

And we know that the syntactical structure of language acts as a formula that allows us to contemplate and discuss an infinite number of concepts and events using a finite number of word signs. So with the same ten words we could have said:

A big brown dog ran away from a frightened cat.

or

A brown cat ran from a big frightened dog.

These are very different concepts altogether.

Language is a Reflection of the Physical World

In a very real sense, language is a pure reflection of the physical universe. Look around. What do you see? The world is made up of "stuff"—you, the couch on which you sit, the floor on which the couch sits, the wall at which the floor ends— all stuff. Where the stuff meets is a boundary. It is the boundaries that make it apparent that the stuff is there. This is the nature of the physical world as met by our senses. The wind blows and then it stops—a boundary; a child cries out and then is silent—a boundary. Based on the physical reality of boundaries, it is no wonder that language is structured as it is. Some of the stuff simply *is* (things or nouns). And then there is all the stuff that the things can do, or can be done to the things (actions/verbs). Then there are the subtle differences or degrees of the stuff. There are brown dogs, big dogs, fat dogs, and small dogs (noun modifiers/adjectives). And of course there are the degrees of the actions. I can run *quickly*, or *slowly* (verb modifiers/adverbs). We could say that language is a tool that man has invented—that it acts as signs or symbols that allow us to talk about things, and events in our world (words)—that there is a formula for combining the signs that allows us an infinite number of possibilities (grammar)—and that the "stuff" taken from language, the information, is conceptualized into a neat little packet.

This packaging aspect of language is where the word 'information' comes from—to 'form' 'within'. The ability to package words into information is a very important aspect of the nature of language. It allows us to conceptualize a lot of data into a neat little box, much like electronic computer technology compresses data, and stores it for later access. Some people are especially good at this. My husband spoke on the phone last week to his father in England for about forty minutes. The conversation was filled with the usual laughter, mixed in with the occasional "oh!" and "uh, huh" and "oh really!" and the odd, "I didn't know that," and even one very long "woooow." When he hung up we sat down to the dinner table and as the salad was passed around I questioned, "So, what's your father up to?" After forty minutes of "oh" and "uh, huh," his answer was surprisingly condensed. "Oh, not much. They're planning a holiday to Florida in November. Dad's golf game is on the up. He sends his love." This ability to compress data makes humans very efficient little bio-computers. Geoff was able to share with me the important parts of a forty minute phone call—I need to have the guest room ready for a November visit from a father-in-law who still loves me. Another skill that humans possess is the ability to bring prior knowledge to their language experiences, making language more than the sum of its parts. Let's use my dinner table tale of my husband's talk with his father as an example. Based on my prior knowledge of my father-in-law and my husband's summary of their talk, I can form an hypothesis that my father -in-law, an avid but average golfer, will arrive in Florida in high spirits and that much of the visit will be spent on the golf course.

The fact is that language is *oh so much more* than any of the definitions mentioned in this chapter or in any of the psychology or linguistics books and research journals you may choose to scour. Language is that thing that most strongly connects us to our fellow man. Through it we can externalize our most precious thoughts and musings, or learn what is in the heart of another. It is the key that allows us, even compels us, to pass on the history of our species, allowing each new generation to learn from the triumphs and tragedies of those who came before.

Does My Child Need to be Taught About the Way Words Go Together?

Much of the accepted use of words is learned through exposure to our language. Children in English speaking countries, for instance, learn that we talk about *big houses* as opposed to *houses big*. They also, hopefully, learn that we use words like *haven't* and *isn't* as opposed to *ain't*. They learn that we *went* fishing as opposed to *goed* fishing. Most of this learning is implicit—it takes place without conscious awareness. Children hear language from parents, teachers, other children and television and radio. It stands to reason that the quality of language heard will reflect the quality of language learned and used. Clearly it's important to expose children to properly spoken language that reflects the physical world in the *accepted* way.   An important question is, will direct *explicit* instruction assist the learning of *accepted* language usage? Will children benefit from good old grammar instruction?

Reber (1989), Berry (1984) and Berry and Dienes (1993) tested the hypothesis that direct explicit instruction would improve language usage. They devised a synthetic language with rules for combining symbols and words, and taught it to students under two controls. One group received direct explicit instruction in the rules for proper usage of the invented language. The other group was exposed to the invented language but received no explicit instruction in the rules of the language. The results clearly indicated that students learned to use the invented language whether they received explicit instruction or not. In the Berry (1984) study researchers found that explicit instruction improved the subjects' knowledge about the rules of the language. On the surface, improved knowledge about the rules of grammar seems a good thing. **But**—the study also showed that the students who received the explicit instruction and acquired knowledge about the rules performed the same or not quite as well as the students who received exposure only, with no explicit instruction in rules.

These findings raise a new question—might explicit instruction impair performance in the use of language? It would seem from this study that although it doesn't hurt much, it certainly doesn't help at all—unless your goal is knowledge about rules rather than performance. This argument is not new to education. The use of explicit instruction in phonetics and grammar has come and gone from classrooms since the inception of compulsory education. This book of course confines the discussion to the use of words (syntax/grammar) rather than sounds (phonetics). The answer to the question, "Do children need specific explicit instruction in grammar in order to speak in the accepted way?" according to the studies mentioned above is **no**. A different question however might be, "Should children be given knowledge about grammatical rules which seem to govern the accepted way of speaking?" The answer to this question is two part. If our society values such knowledge, then children should be taught about it. *But*, it is our responsibility to children to devise ways of giving children that knowledge that do not detract from their use of language—their actual performance. With this in mind it seems prudent to devise methodology that positions explicit instruction in grammar within the context of performance. This is quite doable, but isn't done in most grammar programs.

There are two kinds of grammar programs on the educational market today. The first and most typical are programs that contain errors that the child must correct, blanks that the child must fill in, multiple choices that the child must choose from, parts of speech to be underlined, etc. Children also learn the definition of the various parts of speech by reciting them—*"A noun is a person, place or thing."*

Example of Typical Grammar Instruction

Correct the verb: The girl runned home.   The girl _____ home.
Fill in the correct verb: Today _____ Tuesday.
Choose the correct verb: A dog   sat / sit / sitting   by the boy.
Underline the noun: I like my blue dress.

This kind of instruction is really more of a test than an instructional plan. It contains no methodology for actually teaching the child, other than marking his paper and hoping he gets it right next time. Correction, when it's offered, tends to go like this, "Well Bobby, that's a nice try, but does *Today are Tuesday* sound right to you? We don't speak that way, do we?"

The other grammar instruction that we've seen is much more explicit than this, teaching the linguistic terms for every possible accepted way of connecting words. Children learn, for instance, what an *auxiliary verb* is, how it might or might not connect up to a *prepositional phrase*, and whether that connection gets a comma, a semi-colon or a pat on the back. Years ago I taught this kind of grammar at a community college that offered the course to incoming freshmen who scored poorly on their SATs. I got a real lesson in the usefulness of all I had learned when I started writing books, proudly placing all my commas, semi-colons, etc. in exactly the right places, only to learn that all had changed since 1982 and *these days* we absolutely were not to use a comma between a *this clause* and a *that phrase*— period, end of sentence. That's when I learned that these so-called rules were not actually handed down to some chosen English professor on *Mount Syntax*. When our first book, *Reading Reflex*, was released in Great Britain I learned also that these things were not universal, but varied from English speaking country to English speaking country. And then the ultimate lesson in the impermanence of the rules of grammar reached my consciousness when our second book (this very one) was to be published by a different publisher from our first book, *Reading Reflex*, and we discovered that different publishing houses have different rules, which publishers call *style*.

The important thing that we must teach children about the use of their language is that *meaningful sense* must be conveyed in spoken and written English. Children also need to understand that while fragments and implied thoughts are acceptable in speech, meaningful sense must be conveyed in *complete thoughts* when it is committed to paper. It's fair to say that spoken language is somewhat imprecise, but written language should be perfectly precise. It may well be that knowing what a verb, a noun, a preposition, etc. is will help children recognize a complete from an incomplete thought. So maybe we want to teach them that, but for goodness sake let's keep it in the context of usage—performance. Here's an example of how that's done in the *Language Wise* lessons. In our *Caveman Game* on page 210 for instance, children are asked to talk and eventually write about topics using only nouns, and then only nouns and verbs. This restricted condition demonstrates the usefulness of the various kinds of words, as well as making explicit the reflective nature of language as oral symbols for the things and events in the world around us. We'll play the *Caveman Game* in the next chapter.

Why is There Such Disparity Among the Ability to Use Language Signs?

As we illustrated earlier, our fifteen year old Amanda the daughter is much smarter than Sophie the dog, so Amanda can use many more language signs than Sophie. And as we also illustrated earlier, signs have broader implications for Amanda than for Sophie. When confronted with the sign 'sit', Sophie recognizes the implication that she might get a walk, while the implications for Amanda are much broader, "Let's see, what evil have I done that Mom may have uncovered?" An entire process of reflection follows. Meanwhile Sophie waits patiently for the leash. If the leash doesn't appear in a few minutes, she goes about her business. No further implications occur to her. This disparity is to be expected. After all, Sophie is a dog. But why is there such disparity among humans using language? Why is it that some people can perfectly illustrate their point, while others are left stuttering and groping for the right word? What is the *cause* of this disparity?

Due to the limitations of statistics, linguists, psychologists and other scientists do not like to speak of 'causes', but refer rather to 'correlations' and 'strong correlations' when they report their findings. As we pointed out in chapter one, parents and teachers already feel distanced from their children and students. The 'futility effect' is built on words like 'correlation'. Karl Pearson, one of the founders of modern statistics, said, "Correlation lay on the border of causality." So for the purposes of this book, we'll refer to 'probable reasons' as we speak of the correlational findings.

There are many 'probable reasons' for individual differences in success with language. The most obvious probability is that some people know more words than others (Dunn & Peabody, 1981). Remember that words are tools. Having a poor vocabulary is like having a broken faucet and no 'widget' that fits it—you know what it is you want to say, but you're at a loss for the right words to say it. In some instances you have a widget, but it is the wrong one—you know what you want to say, but you say something entirely different. Or worse still, you don't even know of the existence of 'widgets'—so you don't even conceive of the idea of fixing the faucet.

Another possible reason for disparity in language success is differences in success at forming networks or relationships between words and word groups (Atchison, 1987). Knowing the meaning of the words 'serious' and 'speculative', for instance, is a handy trick, but being able to see the range of possibilities for association between the words is a trick that lends infinite possibilities to their usage. Brown and Berko (1960) discovered that before age seven children asked to respond to word association tasks will almost always offer what might likely be the next word in a sentence, such as "eat—candy." Between the age of seven and the college years, there is a considerable improvement in the ability to generate words that are related by type of function, such as "eat—drink," demonstrating that these older subjects better understand the relationships between words.

In another study showing the improvement in the ability of children to structure language according to relationships, researcher Eve Clark (1974) showed that it isn't until age seven that children can easily define words. When asked the question, "What is a cousin?" younger children answered with statements like, "I have a cousin," while seven year olds answered with, "A cousin is your aunt's child," or "It's when your mom's sister has a child." Clearly their understanding of the relationship of the words 'mother', 'sister', 'aunt' and 'cousin' helped these children to better articulate their answers. It's as if before age seven the first concern of children is how words relate to *them*, and only after age seven do most children begin to consider how words relate to one another. In the *Language Wise* game *Connections* on page 182, we give the child an opportunity to explore the connections between words. Children are given word pairs with no apparent connection and asked to come up with one. So words like *bacon* and *chair* are offered for connection. One ten year old working with a trained *Language Wise* teacher in London came up with an interesting possibility. "They're both edible," he proclaimed proudly. "People eat bacon and termites eat chairs." His teacher, a lecturer at the University of Buckingham, e-mailed me this insight. He was so excited that he wrote in his e-mail, "Ten minutes of Language Wise and these children are ready for their SATs *(student achievement tests are required of all eleven year old children in Great Britain)*."

What is the Role of the Parent in the Child's Understanding of the Nature of Language?

It is an irony of nature that the species who ultimately grow to be the most intelligent on the planet are born with the least amount of intellectual pre-wiring. Only a small amount of the human brain is dedicated to genetically determined behavior and information, as compared to the brains of other species, who appear on the planet with fully functional hunting, eating, grooming, mating and nesting behaviors. These animals spend very little time dependent on their parents. Indeed, no other species has a period of dependency even remotely as long as that of the human child. It is a kind of bargain we cut with nature that we will work very hard and for a long time at raising our children, but the net result will be well worth it. The infancy of Sophie the dog was but a millisecond in my life in comparison to the infancy of Amanda the daughter. Sophie the dog needed no grooming lessons. Her table manners have remained much the same since we adopted her. But Amanda was a bit more of a challenge.

Over the early years of a child's life there is much to be taught and learned, much culture to be passed on, a rich history, the secrets of the sciences, and an assortment of social mores. All of this is possible because the human child is naturally blessed with the treasure of language.

Fortunately for my daughter Amanda, I realized my larger part in the picture while raising my first child. Suspecting he was bright, we had had Rob tested. I remember getting the results and thinking, "Oh good, he's smart. Now I can carry on with the rest of my life." One day on our way home from school Rob announced proudly that his teacher had "...opened up a can of spiders..." at school that day. I was only half attending to this conversation, immersed in adult thoughts, so I assumed this must be a science thing—spiders and all, and said something along the lines of, "that's nice." The next morning, I walked Rob into class, as I sometimes did when I had time, and groping for something to say that would give evidence of my parental involvement, I ventured the question, "Where do you keep the spiders?" The puzzled look on Mrs. Horn's face alerted me to the fact that I had grossly misunderstood, but I was in too deep, so I ventured further, "Rob tells me you got spiders...from a can?" And as soon as I said it, I realized the absurdity of it. Live insects are not packed in cans, she informed me politely, but she would like very much to talk to me after school about Rob's recent behavior problems. **Of course**, behavior problems, cans—spiders—worms—*cans of worms*. Rob had learned the subtle art of cliche, used one incorrectly and mom didn't even bother to notice. Just how deep was the intellectual damage I had inflicted on Rob? Not very—certainly not as deep as imagined by his psychology major mom.

Four years after I condemned my son to a life long cliche disorder, researchers (Penner, 1987) looked at the role of parents in contributing to or inhibiting verbal skills. Penner observed that parent efforts are primarily attempts to communicate effectively rather that deliberate attempts to improve the vocabulary of their children, and that once parent and child can communicate fairly effectively, parental attention to the child's vocabulary development drops off considerably.

Cross-cultural studies also point to parent expectation as a variable in the final result of vocabulary development. In a 1977 study of several cultures, Cole and Scribner found that the ability to recall important information varies considerably across cultures depending upon the expectations of parents in the various cultures.

Anyone who's ever raised an independent child is justified in asking, "Could parent motive and expectation really carry that much weight?" From the moment they learn to crawl, these creatures seem duty bound to get away from us. They wear different clothes from us, listen to different music, eat food that we consider poisonous, ignore us completely in public places, and on the whole seem completely unconcerned with our opinions and desires. How could it be that nature has reserved us this small dominion over their language development? What trick is it that allows us to preserve this last bastion of influence? According to a 1981 study (Price, Hess & Dickson), it may be as simple as *asking*. These researchers found that mothers who asked their children to remember important information and then quizzed them informally later had a much higher success rate than mothers who lacked similar expectations.

As scientific research sometimes does, these studies may contain subtleties that have not been explored. Most parents have high expectations for their children. But are those expectations well formulated? Are parents expressing their expectation clearly to themselves and to their children? What parents need to ask themselves is, "Am I stating my expectations clearly, am I offering something to my child that allows him to meet my expectations," and "Am I responding appropriately when my expectations are not met?"

Ten year old Steven, a *Language Wise* client at the Read America clinic, comes to mind. Steven's parents were in the process of getting a divorce and Steven was in the process of proving that he didn't respect the opinion of either of them. He was brought in for *Language Wise* verbal intelligence therapy be-cause his grades were starting to decline. At intake Steven's mother complained that no matter what she asked him to do, or what she told him, he would ignore her, claiming to have forgotten. She was very concerned that he had a serious re-tention problem. In therapy, Steven was distractable and less than enthusiastic. We spent a lot of time on strategies for vocabulary development. He took to these with ease, and didn't have trouble remembering the new words he learned de-spite his attitude. His mother continued to insist that he forgot everything she asked him to do or told him. As we sometimes do at Read America, I paid a visit to Steven's home after a few months of therapy. The mystery of his memory prob-lem was solved within the first few minutes of my visit. Steven's mother actually never really asked him to do anything. What she did was to apologetically *sug-gest* that he might *consider* doing *this* or *that*. It required some very active self-regulation, but in time Steven's mother was *telling* him what she expected of him in the way of homework, chores and general information, and getting the same success we had been getting at the clinic for some time. In time Steven discov-ered that he could learn a lot from his mom. She taught him to play chess and they became partners in a new hobby—home improvement.

What Other Variables Impact the Outcome of Verbal Intelligence?

In addition to the intention of the parent or teacher and the clear communication of that intention, content of instructional materials may be another important variable to vocabulary development. Numerous studies have shown that cur-riculum content impacts memory of material. In a study conducted by Flavel and Wellman (1977) researchers found that until age nine children could recall with equal accuracy lists of words that could be categorized easily such as /dog/chair/couch/pig/table/cow/lamp/cat/ and lists of words that could not be cat-egorized easily such as /blue/cat/happy/sit/pen/apple/Tuesday/park/. After age nine, the age at which children begin to categorize with consistent success, chil-dren had a much higher rate of success at recalling lists of words that could be categorized. This may indicate that the relationship of words is used as an aid to memory.

In another study, Deborah Best and Peter Ornstein (1986) asked an experi-mental group of nine year olds to sort easily categorizable items, while the con-trol group was asked to sort items that were not easily categorizable. They found that the experimental group later performed better than the control group at sorting materials that were not easily categorizable. The experimental group was also better than the control group at recall tests about the material they sorted. This offers important evidence that simple exposure to categories may tend to cause the learner to set up an organizational structure for later use. Both the experimental and control groups were asked to teach first graders how to remember. The experimental group who had been exposed to the easily categorizable items was more likely to mention the importance of organization when telling the younger children how to remember.

These nine year olds saw the value in making their young charges aware of their own part in the learning process. This kind of awareness is called 'meta-awareness' or 'metacognition'—being aware of what strategies you used to learn. Children show signs of metacognition earlier than you might think. In a study conducted by DeLoache, Cassidy and Brown (1985) researchers observed that when an object was hidden from two year old subjects they would return to the last place they had seen the object—exactly what adults do in the same situation. Although research with children so young is difficult to analyze, it would seem that these toddlers were *trying* to remember. They were *thinking* about *thinking*. According to Piaget's follower, John Flavel, children have fairly well established metacognitive skills by about age seven. For instance, they are able to predict with high accuracy the number of words that they can recall from a list. *Language Wise* activities in section two will help your child become more proficient at categorizing information and learning new vocabulary.

How Do I Put What I Know to Work for My Child?

We know that children learn language skills more easily when parents place expectations on them. We know that the categorical and functional relationship of words is a reflection of the physical universe. We know that conscious awareness or 'metacognition' of the categorical and functional relationship of words is important to understanding and being able to express information about the world. As the nine year old tutors in the last section discovered, these are opportunities for curriculum development. They are windows into the verbal landscape of the child's mind. Are parents and teachers recognizing and using curriculum opportunities as they work to develop the verbal skills of their children and students?

In developing the *Language Wise* program, we isolated the challenges, took what we know about the nature of language and attempted to simplify them. For an example let's look at the challenge of vocabulary development. We know that words are invented by man. We know that words are signs that help children make sense of the world around them. With this we can begin to develop an activity. Let's start with the goals.

Goals

1. To help your child see the symbolic nature of words.

2. To help your child to see the usefulness of words as symbols or signs.

A likely activity might be to use new vocabulary in sentences so that she can figure out the word based on what she *does* know about the environment. With this idea we can add another goal to our activity.

3. To help your child to see that she can use what she knows about the world as a key to the meanings of new words.

Keeping these goals in mind, we can begin to structure a presentation format.

Presentation

1. Invite your child to play a game of 'word detective' with you.

2. Tell her the mystery word is 'snat'. Ask her if she has any idea what it means. When she says no, or starts guessing wrong, point out that she can't possibly know what it means yet, because you just invented it and the meaning is in your head.

3. Explain that if you say the word in a sentence, she might be able to figure out what the word means. Say the sentence:

The <u>snat</u> barked at the mailman.

4. She'll likely say that a snat is like a dog. When she does, ask her to tell you how she figured out the answer.

5. Continue on with more nonsense words. The next time you play the game start with nonsense words and then move to real words.

Age Appropriateness

5 years to adult—vary difficulty of words

We know that life is not always perfect and that sometimes even the simplest problems present difficulty for children, so our lesson will need a section on correcting errors. There are a few places where things could go wrong in this activity. Let's have a look at one.

Correcting Problems

After hearing the sentence, your child still doesn't know the meaning of the word.

To help her see how to find out, ask her, "What do we know about snat?" She should offer that it barks. If she doesn't, tell her, "Well, the sentence said that the snat barked, so we know that a snat is a thing that barks."

Let's play our game at the adult level. By playing the game yourself, you can better experience how it will help your child to accomplish the goals we've laid out. I'll be the teacher and you be the student. I'm going to assume that you're pretty smart. I'm basing this assumption on the fact that you bought our book. So, assuming that you're smart, I'm going to choose some really difficult words from my dictionary, make up sentences using them and see if you can figure out what they mean. You're on your honor not to peek ahead at the answers. After you read each sentence write down what you think the word might mean. You can define it with a synonyms or with a descriptive sentence.

1. As the sun set in the west, George rose from the table and suggested a post - <u>prandial</u> walk._____

   _____

2. Sam's <u>poltroonery</u> at the meeting led his boss to decide that Sam was not the man for a job that demands guts and nerves of steel. _____

   _____

3. His <u>jocundity</u> was evident as he sang and told stories of the good old days.

   _____

   _____

4. Given the bitter chill Rolf was glad he had worn a <u>semmit</u> as well as a wool shirt and tweed overcoat. _____

   _____

5. His <u>jockery</u> gained him control of the company, and many mistrusting enemies. _____

   _____

Starting with number one let's review how you came to your answers.

> *As the sun set in the west, George rose from the table and suggested a*
> *post-<u>prandial</u> walk.*

If you already knew the meaning of prandial, good for you. But if you didn't, your first step should have been to ask, "What *do* I know from the sentence?"

> *It's late in the day*
> *George is leaving the table*
> *What do we do at the table late in the day?*
> *Eat dinner*
> *Prandial has to do with dinner.*

So you try your hypothesis:

> *As the sun set in the west, George rose from the table and suggested a*
> *post-<u>dinner</u> walk.*

And then you make adjustments so it sounds like language you've heard before:

> *As the sun set in the west, George rose from the table*
> *and suggested an after-<u>dinner</u> walk.*

Number two is even easier.

> *Sam's <u>poltroonery</u> at the meeting led his boss to decide that Sam was*
> *not the man for a job that demands guts and nerves of steel.*

What do you know from the sentence?

> *Sam doesn't have guts and nerves of steel.*
> *What is it called when you have no guts?*
> *cowardice*
> *Sam's <u>cowardice</u> at the meeting led his boss to decide that Sam was*
> *not the man for a job that demanded guts and nerves of steel.*

Let's do number three.

> *His <u>jocundity</u> was evident as he sang and told stories of the good old days.*

What do you know from the sentence?

> *Something about him showed when he sang and told stories.*
> *How do we feel when we sing and tell stories?*
> *Happy, joyous*

His joy was evident as he sang and told stories of the good old days.

Let's try number four.

Given the bitter chill Rolf was glad he had worn a semmit as well as a wool shirt and tweed overcoat.

What do you know from the sentence?

A semmit is something that keeps you warm.
A semmit is not a coat, or shirt.
What's left?
An undershirt. A semmit is an undershirt.
Given the bitter chill Rolf was glad he had worn an undershirt as well as a wool shirt and tweed overcoat.

And let's do number five.

His jockery gained him control of the company, and many mistrusting enemies.

What do you know from the sentence?

He got what he wanted by being untrustworthy.
People who can't be trusted are dishonest. They cheat.
His cheating gained him control of the company, and many mistrusting enemies.

Can't All Children Do This?

Playing *Word Detective* offers your child more than just quality time with you, it offers him the opportunity to see that he can use what he already knows about the world around him to discover the meanings of new words. This is a skill he will take with him through life, allowing him to acquire new vocabulary wherever and whenever it appears. The simplicity of this skill may tempt you to think, "Oh, that's so easy. Surely all children *do* that." Don't make this critical error with your child. All children do not *get* this simple skill. Indeed many do not get it in adulthood. We've worked with many children who could communicate perfectly well, and received Bs and even As at school, who lacked this simple skill to unlock word meanings that were not among the words they heard over and over again. To these clients the meaning of a new word was completely inaccessible.

In a study conducted at the Read America clinic, we read a passage to seven children age eight to fourteen whose scores on the Peabody Picture Vocabulary Test (PIATr) were between six and thirty-six months below their actual age. The passage contained a target word that they had missed on the test. The passage was constructed to reveal the meaning of the target word in two separate sentences, much like the sentences on page 53, but these were words that a child of that age would be expected to know. After hearing the passage containing the clues, and then being asked again at the end of the passage what the target word meant, all of the children responded with statements like, "I don't know that word." One young man said, "If you tell me what it means I'll remember." To these children word meanings are just arbitrary bits of information that they should learn by rote and remember. One week later each of the children received a lesson in *Word Detective*, just as you did on the previous pages, and then played the game for ten minutes or so with a therapist. After completion of the session another therapist read the same passage to them and then asked them the meaning of the target word which they had gotten wrong the week before. Though their definitions of the target words did not read like a dictionary, they were accurate and descriptive. Let's play another game!

As we mentioned earlier in the chapter the ability to see possible relationships between words is a very useful skill. Unfortunately, like the ability to unlock word meanings, not everyone can easily see the relationships between words. Let's find out if your skills go in this direction. I'm going to tell you two words, and I want you to tell me something they might have in common. There isn't one designated correct answer. There are lots of possibilities. OK—here goes.

cat—dog _____

_____

newspaper—kerosene _____

_____

spoon—hair spray_____

_____

sparkplug—rubber band_____

_____

Arkansas—bagpipes_____

_____

How did you do? That Arkansas one was hard, wasn't it? We spent some time looking through the files of *Language Wise* clients and picked some of our favorite answers to share with you.

cat—dog   *Bobby (9) They both have fleas.*
Sarah (11) They both go to the vet.
Alice (6) They don't come in blue.

newspaper—kerosene   *Sarah (11) You can start fires with them.*
Stella (8) You can read them.
Brinnea (18) They both have a bad smell.

spoon—hair spray   *Jason (13) WalMart sells them both.*

sparkplug—rubber band   *Alice (6) My dad has them both in his toolbox.*
Bobby (9) They can make airplanes go.

Arkansas—bagpipes   *David (12) They both have pipes.*
Alice (6) They both have bags.

Life is a Package of Reflexes and Learned Reflexes

Hopefully, having played *Word Detective* and *Categories* as a student has helped you to appreciate the value of playing these activities with your child as a means of establishing solid strategies for discovering new vocabulary in the world each day, so that building vocabulary becomes part of his daily routine. As I parent like you, I know how frustrating it can be when your child encounters something he doesn't know (like a new word) and he just moves around it. Lessons like these change all that, establishing automatic strategies that will be in place as all those new words make their way into his world. These games are among the complete *Language Wise* activities included in section two. I'll caution you that although playing these games is more effective than not playing them, in order to reach the expectations that I'm sure you have for your child, the games need to become part of your way of responding to your child. In this regard *Language*

Wise is as much a therapy for you as for your child. As we've pointed out in the sub-title for this section, life is a package of reflexes and learned reflexes—strategies. Your child has a natural propensity to learn language. It's like a reflex. He may not however have very well developed strategies for doing that. That's your job. You want your child to become a *word detective*. You want him to leave no stone unturned in discovering the meaning of words he doesn't know. Your child has two mothers, 'Mother Nature' and *Mom*. Mother Nature blessed him with reflexes. Teaching him strategies is your job. Mother Nature's job is done. Yours is just beginning. If you do a really good job, his strategies will be almost as automatic as his reflexes.

CHAPTER FOUR

AWAY WITH WORDS
FROM VOCABULARY TO COMPREHENSION

In this chapter you will learn

Norms in language development, and how to beat them.

What a 'script' is.

How comprehension works with vocabulary.

Elaboration as an instructional technique.

How to question for maximum instructional value.

How contemporary reading content may be dumbing down your child.

As children begin to grow and develop and have more sophisticated thoughts they don't always have the words to express them. This example comes to us from a primary teacher in Kent, England, whose young son, age five, had just such a problem. His mom had sent him off to bed after he had demonstrated some rather sloppy table manners. When she went to check on him an hour or so later she found this note taped to his bedroom door.

Dear Mommy,
I hate you.

Love,
Andrew

The way that children learn language gives us a remarkably clear window into how we might design and direct their language development later in childhood. Just before his first birthday an infant begins to understand words. Within weeks of this he begins to use words. His first words are nouns that he sees in the world around him, then verbs, then modifiers. By the time a child reaches the age

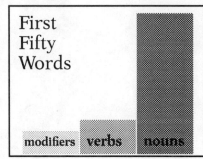

First Fifty Words

modifiers verbs nouns

of eighteen months he has learned his first fifty or so words. According to a 1973 study conducted by Katherine Nelson, approximately sixty-five percent of these early words are nouns, thirteen percent are verbs and nine percent are adjectives and adverbs. As we discussed in chapter three each of these kinds of words reflects what the child sees in the world around him—nouns, *doing* verbs in degrees which *modify* the nouns and verbs. The order of occurrence of these early words is evidence that the young child has an innate sense of syntax, or the various functions of words that reflect the physical world. If used correctly this information gives us tremendous insight into how to instruct children in language arts. Another bit of evidence comes to us from clinical studies which show that babies will become agitated and upset if inanimate objects in their physical world begin to fly around the room on a piece of monofilament wire. Likewise, they become agitated and cry if humans walking through a room should suddenly freeze and move no more. Babies seem just to know that there are *things* (we adults like to think of these as nouns) and the *things* perform *actions* (we adults call these verbs). The mere fact that children are able to perceive word boundaries at all is quite a feat. Anyone who's ever heard a foreign language being spoken knows how difficult it is to determine where one word ends and another begins. Spoken language takes its pauses between syllables, not words. And often the sounds from one spoken word appear in another spoken word. Let's look at an English example. "This Saturday I'll let my dog Sophie have a run in the park." A baby listening to this sentence, trying to find word boundaries to attend to and attach meaning to, might think you said, "Thi sat erd ay I let myd ogs oph ie have a ru nin the park," or "This aterday I let my dogs ophie have a ru nin the park." Take a minute and read all three sentences. They sound about the same. How does an infant work out which sounds make words? According to one theory he listens for consistency and builds frequency patterns, sorting and categorizing sounds as he goes. Wow! What a huge undertaking for a baby.

Richard Burton (the explorer not the actor) spent decades doing this sort of thing on far continents with aboriginal languages. And he could already speak a language! In a study conducted by Marsha Clarkson in 1983, it was discovered that two day old babies can discriminate between the phonemes 'i' and 'a'. By one month they can discriminate consonants as well as adults. Babies are so good at discriminating words and mimicking their parents, that in a 1984 study, researchers (DeBoysson-Bardies, et al.) found that strangers can determine the country of origin of six to ten month old babies from a recording of their babbling.

Once the child has begun to sort out the words from the sounds and the syllables, he starts learning words. According to a 1985 study (Carey), children hear a word, draw an inference about the meaning, try it on Mom or some other significant adept speaker, and gauge the effectiveness. His first fifty words go quite a long way for the novice speaker. He becomes a master at using single words as entire sentences. We call these one word sentences *holophrases*. You might call him a minimalist. A sixteen month old at the grocery store with Mom might be seen pointing at the candy display and saying "canny." This single word is quickly and easily understood by Mom to mean something along the lines of, "excuse me Mother dear, but could you be so good as to fetch me that Baby Ruth bar... the giant size please." A couple of weeks later when Mom has just read an article about the harmful effects of sugar on babies, and baby sends the standard request, "canny", Mom says, "not today" and continues unloading the grocery cart. Baby attempts a new word that has been known to get results when action is needed— "gee." So the command expands from "canny" to "gee canny." We call these two to three word sentences *telegraphic phrases*. Mom, easily impressed, is so pleased with baby's advanced grammatical prowess that she does indeed "gee canny," complete with a big, warm, adoring smile. A few months later baby and mommy are in the same store and baby offers the standard command which is now pronounced with more precision, "gimme canny." Mom offers a modest lollipop and the thanks she gets is tears and a sucker thrown to the floor. Having given up a perfectly good career for this child, mom is understandably confused and hurt. She tries another color sucker but receives the same response. Finally, in frustration, baby discards screams for words and says, "gimme **big** canny." Mom now gets the point. Baby wants one of those great big chocolate bars on the top shelf. And once again, impressed by his obvious genius in being able to construct this eloquent turn of phrase, she hands it over. The moral to the story?—*Thought is father to the word, or in this example—thought is* *father to the chocolate bar.* And so it goes, word by word, need by need, the child's vocabulary grows.

My Child Had a Great Vocabulary at Five
But Now Fails His Vocabulary Tests

According to Durkin (1989) learning new words is largely an unconscious event. Durkin references a study conducted by Carey (1978) which reveals a phenomenon Carey termed *fast mapping*, a process in which children are able to incorporate a new word after only a brief exposure. Dockrell and Campbell (1986) tested *fast mapping* in a similar study in which they exposed children to nonsense words using the words as if they had a specific meaning. They then tested retention of the word in two ways. When given an implicit test—"Does the word make sense in this sentence?"—the children were accurate. When they asked the children for explicit information about the word—a definition—the children performed poorly. This isn't surprising. We asked thirty-two students age seven to sixteen to give us a definition for the word 'mop'. We broke their answers into three distinct cohorts:

1. **an example** such as, *"You wash a floor with it."*
2. **a synonym** such as, *"It's like a broom."*
3. **a description** such as, *"It's a stick with hairy white strings on the end."*

The distribution of the cohorts appears here in a chart.

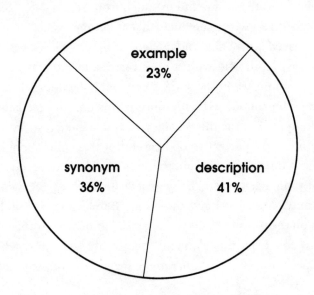

We then asked eleven classroom teachers of children ages eight to ten to rate the answers as acceptable or unacceptable as a definition of a *mop*. Not one of the thirty-two definitions was accepted by a majority of the eleven teachers asked. Next we asked seventeen teachers, none of whom were in the previous group of eleven, to provide a definition of a *mop*. The teachers answered almost identically to the children, with one important difference. In all but one of the definitions the teachers offered, more than one kind of definition was used. For instance they offered an example *and* a description, or a description *and* a synonym. Here's a typical teacher's definition for *mop*—*A mop is a thing for cleaning floors. It is made from a stick with cotton fiber on one end.* A peek in the dictionary tells us that a mop is *a bundle of course yarn or cloth fastened at the end of a stick and used for cleaning floors.* It could be said that the use of a word is for the speaker and the definition of a word is for the listener. If this is so, it stands to reason that children aren't as good at defining words as they are at using them.

One way to improve children's ability to understand the meaning of words is to help them see the various ways to talk about words, to define them. We devised a lesson called *Definitions* for doing just that. The child is invited to choose a word from a stack of words. The child has to offer three ways to define the word. First he offers a physical description of the word, followed by an example of the use, and finally a synonym or similar word. After these three steps, he develops a single definition including all the information from the three steps. The other players write down their guesses about the word when he's done. He gets a point for each correct guess generated by his definition.

Other lessons take up where this lesson leaves off. *Telling Tools* requires the student to talk and then write about a topic using the following *telling tools*—description, example, sequence, parts and categories, comparison and contrast, cause and effect, fact, what if, anecdote, and quote. The example taken from the lesson on page 215 demonstrates all of the following in reference to *an egg*.

> **example-** Eggs are pretty easy to break. If I dropped one from the roof of my house onto my sidewalk it would definitely break, but if an egg rolls off the kitchen table and onto the carpet it might not break.

> **sequence-** Some eggs are good to eat. They should be cooked first. One way to cook an egg is to hard boil it. First you put the egg in a pot. Next you fill the pot until the egg is covered and the

water is an inch higher than the egg. Then you put the pot on a high heat until it starts to boil. When the water boils, turn the stove off and cover the pot. Leave the egg in the water for twenty minutes. Cooling the egg is important too. Pour all the water into the sink. Place the pot in the sink and run cool water into the pot for about three minutes. The cool water helps cool the egg without cracking it. Leave the egg sitting in water for at least thirty minutes. Now you can place the egg in the refrigerator. After the egg has chilled for an hour or so it's ready to eat.

parts and categories- There are four parts of a chicken egg. The shell is the hard part on the outside of the egg. The shell membrane is inside the shell. The membrane is soft. It is a thin layer of skin. The egg white is inside the membrane. The white protects the yolk from being damaged. The yolk is inside the white. The yolk is the part of the egg that will turn into a chicken if the egg is fertilized.

compare and contrast- Chicken eggs are not very big. They are smaller than a baseball, but bigger than a jumbo marble. They are not sphere shaped like balls and marbles. They are shaped a little bit like a football. However, unlike a football, they are not the same size at each end. One end comes to a small, round point like a football, but the other end is more rounded like a round ball.

cause and effect- When an egg is inside a mother animal its shell is soft and round, but when it comes out of the mother animal its shell is hard and elongated. The change in the egg is caused by two things. The shape is changed as the egg is pushed out of the mother's body. The egg becomes hard outside the mother's body because it dries in the air.

fact- Eggs are high in protein, which is good for you, but they are also high in fat, which is bad for some people. If you have a heart condition or a gallstone you should not eat many eggs.

what if- If dinosaurs were still on earth they would lay giant eggs. We could use their eggs to feed all the poor and starving people in the world. One dinosaur egg would probably feed about twenty people. But where would we keep the dinosaurs? They could get loose and kill the starving people instead of saving them.

anecdote- I had a friend who told me that he went to a museum and saw a dinosaur egg fossil. He said it was bigger than a football.

quote- My doctor said, "You need more protein. You should have two eggs each day."

One Man's Dog is Another Man's Cow

As need demands the young child adds new words to his vocabulary through a process of experimentation (Herbert & Clark, 1977). In the spirit of experimentation, the young child *underextends* words. So his dog's name, for instance, might be used to reference all dogs. Eventually he learns a more appropriate word—'doggy'. Next he experiments with *overextending* the word, so when he sees a cow, he calls it 'doggy'.

A 1973 study conducted by Eva Clark observed that children overextend based on physical attributes, such as the 'doggy/cow' example above. A later study (1978) by Katherine Nelson found that children also overextend based on function. The first time a child encounters a stool, for instance, and his daddy lifts him on to it, he may label it 'chair', because its function is to seat people. Our *Language Wise* lesson *Systematic Reasoning* encourages children to seek systems of analysis, allowing them to bounce back and forth between functional analysis and attributional analysis, and thereby allowing them much more flexibility in how they uncover meaning and use words. We know that young children are capable of this based on research conducted by developmental psychologists Ellen Markman and Jeanne Hutchinson. Two and three year olds were given an assortment of utensils and other materials. The researchers showed each child in turn a set of wooden tongs and asked them to, "find a 'biff' like this." They used a nonsense word in order to learn if the children would choose a function or attribute in making their choice of another 'biff'. The set of materials contained other tongs made of metal and plastic, and other items also made of wood. The children chose tongs made of other materials in locating a 'biff', showing that they understand and can use function in making choices where no exact match is available. The researchers repeated the experiment with another group of children. This time they had no other tongs in the set of materials and stated the question, "*can* you find another 'biff'?" The children chose items made of wood, the same material as the tongs. These studies indicate that children are capable of conceiving of functional or attributional relationships at a very early age, juggling between the two as needed in order to organize the available information. In this lesson, the child is asked if item one is more like item two or item three. The goal as stated is to encourage the child to be flexible in his use of functional and attributional variables. Let's do one now. Jot down your answer and then offer an explanation of your decision.

Is juice more like fruit or water? _____

Why?_____

_____

_____

_____

_____

Did you notice yourself going back and forth between physical attributes like, *it's like fruit because they both grow on trees, contain sugar, start out the same—* and functional attributes like *it's like water because you drink them both.* Why would you need to do this kind of lesson with your child if children naturally think in terms of attributes and functions? Because sometimes things don't go as well as you might hope.

Older children and adults who haven't developed good language practices *under-* and *over*extend language and concepts just like very young children. And sometimes they're educated people. Watching the news a few months back, I heard the newscaster say to a firefighter, "I understand the fire has spread south. Can you *extrapolate* on that for us?" While I was working with seventeen year old Will about a month ago he said, "I'd like to major in business but my mom is trying to *distract* me from it." A contestant on a popular game show was talking about his daughter's new husband and said, "We like him an *extreme* lot." These older children and adults have stopped viewing their language experiences as experiments. They no longer wait for feedback and adjust what they've said accordingly. They stumble forward, using words that are too narrow or too broad to work well in the context in which they've used them or are just plain wrong.

Perhaps early language tests could single out children at risk of becoming like those adults mentioned above. According to language researcher Roger Brown, the best estimate of early development is 'mean length of utterance'. This is the number of morphemes in a child's phrase. A morpheme is the smallest unit of meaning in a language. So in our example above, 'canny' contains a mean length of utterance (MLU) of one, while 'gee canny' contains an MLU of two, 'gimme canny' contains an MLU of three, and 'gimme big canny' contains an MLU of four. If, as language researchers believe, the length of a child's early phrases is a marker of his development, parents should indeed be proud of such strides, and should encourage longer and longer phrases. Considerable research has shown that while parents don't actually correct the speech of their toddlers, they do tend to reward longer sentences with joy, presumably shaping the development of increasingly complex sentences. A 1985 study (Bohannen & Warren-Leubcker) found that at any given time in a child's development the parent uses slightly more complex and longer sentences than the child. There is no evidence that this is a conscious plan of parents, and in fact may be more of a reaction than a good parenting practice.

The parent who wants to actually drive his child's language development might consider staging scenarios in which the child is inspired to stretch his MLU just a bit. Let's go back to our first trip to the grocery store with baby and Mom. Our sixteen month old baby is fussing for 'canny' with an MLU of one. In our continued scenario it took a few months for him to extend to an MLU of four—'gimme big canny'. This might have been accomplished sooner with some creative parenting. "Oh, you want 'candy'. Let's see, which candy do you want? *This* one, or *that* one (pointing to two different kinds in turn)." This kind of interaction encourages the development of new words, such as *this* and *that*. This kind of intentional attempt to develop language sooner often results in longer utterances at an earlier age. Is this valuable, or just a source of delight for anxious parents and language researchers? Actually it's very valuable. Linguists and speech and language specialist teachers consider MLU to be the highest indicator of vocabulary in later childhood. The child who offers a longer than average MLU at two years will be the teenager with the higher vocabulary at thirteen. So baby's turn of phrase does indeed matter. What would happen if the parent actually did make conscious efforts to improve the child's vocabulary? As we pointed out in the last chapter, the parent intentionally training the child in skills not yet considered essential is an instructional ingredient that accounts for much of the child's intelligence over and above the norm.

Parents trying to increase their child's MLU should understand that certain principles and limitations apply. Remember from chapter two that language is a reflection of the physical universe. The child's first words—nouns, verbs and modifiers—are the stuff of the world around him. As we've said it's no surprise that these appear in his language. The fact that nouns are the first to appear is natural as the people and things of the world are most perceivable to the young child. That verbs appear next in his speech is also not surprising as it would follow that once the child can label people and things, he might start to notice what those people and things are *doing*—"train <u>go</u>." The use of modifiers next allows the developing child to speak with more precision about the people and things in his world and the actions they take—"<u>big</u> train go <u>fast</u>." These components of language can be encouraged at earlier ages by parents' interaction with the developing child in two ways:

1. Speak more to your child. Offer lots and lots of meaningful labels for the people, things, actions and modifiers in your child's world. As he grows older offer new labels for words he already knows.
   "Yes that's a pretty flower, but do you know what kind?"
   "Yes it is a nice day, in fact it's a *glorious* day."
2. Expect more from your child. Expect your child to offer more than single holophrases as he grows out of infancy. When he asks for something require clarity. As he learns the names of things offer modifiers as well. So when he says "doggy," answer with, "Yes, that's right. *Big* doggy." As he reaches middle childhood expect more still. Don't settle for one word answers and cliches.

On the other hand, there are some things that are not reasonable expectations for the very young child. Children under the age of two, when asked to repeat the phrase, "The dog chased the cat," will respond with, "Dog chase cat," omitting the auxiliary words and the past tense marker. There is evidence that these early omissions of certain word types and word parts are based on developmental limitations. According to a 1986 study (Reich), these words and word parts are simply too abstract for the young child. They're invisible denotations of the relationships between words. There is no physical basis for them in the real world. They exist only in the mind of the speaker. Some languages don't even contain such words. In Russian for instance, "dog chased cat" is correct usage. Russian contains no articles. One must infer whether it is just *any* cat (*a* cat), or a particular cat (*the* cat) being chased. Developing children from cultures that do use articles will learn to use them by acculturation. This process takes time, but it also requires that the child has matured enough to manage the more abstract and invisible concept of *any* or a *particular* cat. This developmental milestone occurs naturally at about the third birthday (McNeill, 1970).

In another study (Brown, 1973) researchers found that children tend to grasp and use such abstract language markers at slightly varying ages, but in the same order of appearance between the ages of two and a half and five. The order of appearance is shown on the chart.

Early Language Acquisition

___ 5

– Past tense irregulars like 'ran' as
– opposed to 'runned'

– Articles such as 'the' and 'a'
___ 4

– Proper use of the verb to be
– such as 'was' and 'are'

– Possessives
___ 3

– Regular past tense such as 'I jumped' as
– opposed to 'I jump'

– Pluralization
___ 2 The prepositions 'in' and 'on'
– 'Ing' to denote present tense

–

___ 1

–

The predictable order of appearance of these milestones is further evidence that language unfurls as the mind can understand the specific kind of unit of meaning. Present tense *ing*, for instance, appears before past tense *ed*. What the child sees, hears, feels, smells and tastes is present tense. Once gone, an experience requires memory to be considered and is, in this sense, more complex than that which is happen*ing* right now.

As children run language experiments, they seek patterns on which to build hypotheses. When the patterns don't work, young children make predictable errors, saying things like, "I runned" instead of "I ran." That children make pattern based errors with this irregular break from the *ed* past tense marker reveals that children have a basic understanding that the past tense word is associated with the present tense word. If children didn't understand this, and thought that each tense was a novel word, they would not make these pattern based errors.

A Wug is a Wug is a Wug

A classic 1958 study (Berko) set out to test this very hypothesis. Researchers looked at the formation of plurals using invented words that children had never heard before. They wanted to find out if children learn plurals as new words, or if they learn new words as variations of the singular word they already know, with a standard pluralization structure attached. In other words, does the young child who knows 'cat' learn that the sound 's' attached to the end of 'cat' means that there are more than one of them, or does the child learn 'cats' as a new word with a new meaning—"more than one of the animal I call 'cat'." Researchers showed four and five year olds the following picture and said, "this is a wug."

They then showed them several of the same figure in one picture and asked the children, "what's this?"

The children identified the picture as "wugs," offering critical evidence that young children form hypotheses about the structure of words and then extend that structure to all words—even if they've never heard the word before. In this way, children can be thought of as little scientists, forming and testing hypotheses and adding to their language repertoire as they do. In a 1979 study (Slobin) researchers found that when children encounter irregular word structures, such as 'I go' becoming 'I went' rather than 'I goed', these irregular structures are eventually taken into the repertoire.

Does this system ever fail? Are there children who don't learn about language in this way? Do some children miss the point? There are otherwise normal children who fail to use predictable word structures with consistent accuracy even after years of exposure. These children reach the age of seven or eight using sentences like, "Next week we goed at the beach," and "I are hungry." They mix tenses, failing to accomplish subject-verb agreement, overgeneralize word structure well past the age of five, by which time their peers have accomplished consistently accurate grammar, and use inappropriate prepositions such as 'I go at' rather than 'I go to'. These children beg important instructional questions. *What causes these children to miss critical patterns in their language? Do these children ever catch up to their peers? How could these problems be prevented?*

Itard's Wolf Child

There have been historical events that have offered us rare answers to some of these questions. In the last few years of the eighteenth century in the Aveyron Province of France, a young boy was found in the woods, in the care of wolves who had apparently raised him from infancy when, it is assumed, he was abandoned or orphaned. This child, thought to be about six or seven years old, came to be known as the Wolf Child of Aveyron. The boy was soon committed to the care of Jean Marc Gaspard Itard, a physician from the Institute for Deaf Mutes in Paris. Subjected to the most rigorous testing of the era, the wolf boy was thought to be of normal intelligence. Having been raised exclusively by wolves, he possessed no human language, but only the growls and howls of his wolf family. Itard spent many years with the wolf child, attempting to teach him language—though little success was made. Although the wolf child was able to learn many words to label the things in his world, he was never able to master anything but the most basic grammar. Since the work of Itard, other such children have been found having been isolated from human language. In each case, the development of language had been critically impaired if the child discovered was older than five or six years of age.

Hearing loss during the sensitive period for language acquisition, though certainly not as devastating as isolation, can cause mild to severe language delays. Many children suffer hearing loss without their parents' knowledge for many years. Do these children learn to process the critical words that lead to meaning, coasting over the articles, prepositions and connectors? Their early speech would imply that they do. Children whose language is delayed by hearing loss speak in telegraphic sentences for some time after the hearing loss is corrected. Eventually they learn to speak normally, but whether their seemingly normal speech is mimicked scripts, sounding much like the words they now hear, or fluid language is a question as yet unanswered by the field of applied linguistics. The *Language Wise* lessons are especially powerful at breaking up scripts and replacing them with meaningful interactive language. In field testing of these lessons thirty-eight percent of teachers using *Language Wise* worked with children with learning disabilities. These teachers reported improvements equaling those of their colleagues working with normal populations.

A Sensitive Period for Language Development

Stories like that of the Wolf Child of Aveyron and extensive cases of children suffering early hearing loss offer convincing evidence that there is a sensitive period for the development of grammatical syntax. Linguists believe that if children are not exposed to the grammatical structure of a human language early in life, they will never reach mastery of that structure. But what of children who *are* exposed to human language yet lag critically behind their peers? It may be that these children miss many of the subtleties of language and pass beyond the sensitive period of language development without having reached mastery. This idea might explain why some children remain outside of the range considered to be normal development in language related tasks. Many of these children apparently catch up in time, but do they really? Studies of such language delayed children have shown that though their sentence structure does appear to enter the normal range by early adulthood, their overall verbal abilities remain low. Is this a *cause* of their initial language delays, or is their low overall language ability a *result* of having missed the point early on? Would these young adults have reached higher eventual scores in language related tasks had they made early connections about the structure of language within the sensitive period for such development?

What are the particular mechanics of language that these children miss? It may be that they never become intimate with the notion that words and word parts carry meaning—that these smallest units of meaning (morphemes) are embedded in complete thoughts. It may be that these children operate only in and on complete thoughts—clauses and sentences that contain a subject and an action—with insufficient regard to the smaller units of meaning within these clauses and sentences. This would explain why these children can make sense (of a kind) of sentences like 'I goed at the beach', but fail to notice (as their peers have) that there is another word that is used when 'I have gone' and that word is 'went', and that one goes 'to' and not 'at' the beach. These children may find it difficult to manipulate units of meaning beyond those that directly reflect the physical universe—units like articles, prepositions and the parts of words that allow subtle changes, like 's' to pluralize, or suffixes that mark a word as a concept as opposed to a verb such as changing 'pack' to 'pack<u>age</u>' or 'delete' to 'dele<u>tion</u>'.

Yoursguys's and Other Scripts

An adult whose language skills fall on the low end of the bell curve may sound fairly normal to the casual observer. She can communicate well enough, and no longer says, "I goed at the beach," but she does have some tortured sentence structure and word usage. My family and I recently traveled to San Francisco to train a group of teachers in *Language Wise* techniques. After training we headed down the beautiful California coast for a few days' vacation. On the first day we stopped in at a lovely seaside restaurant for an early dinner. The hostess greeted us, taking our name and the number in our party. She apologized saying, "There'll be a twenty minute wait 'time.' I'll call you when 'yoursguys's' table is ready." This young lady seemed not to understand that 'your' can be used to refer to one or many, so our entire family could have a table called 'your table'. Her solution to this dilemma was to make us—who she apparently thought of as 'you guys'—'yoursguys' and to denote that the table would belong to us, she added not one, but two 's' possessives, making the table 'yoursguys's'. Much of our dinner conversation was spent in hushed tones trying to determine whether the table was now usguys's, ourguys's, or oursguy's. After much whispered debate, we finally settled on oursguys's. In addition to the tortured way in which the table was denoted as ours, the hostess failed to realize that a twenty minute wait would, naturally, require time, and therefore needn't be called a 'wait *time*'.

Later that night our daughter Mandy stubbed her toe on a suitcase poorly situ-
ated in our hotel room. Over breakfast the next morning she proclaimed with
much glee that she had a bad case of 'toe stubbage'. When asked for an explanation she explained that, "Toe stubbage is what you have when you have stubbed
your toe." She was (we hope) taking what she knows about the structure of
words and *playing* with language. When her father teased her, arguing that
'stubbage' isn't a word, she answered with a playful (we think), "Of course, my
mistake, I meant to say 'stubbation'."

Yoursguys's is certainly a blatant example of poor word usage. I recently
heard a more subtle misuse of language on a television advertisement. While a
shiny new red sports utility vehicle sped along a stretch of oceanfront highway, a
voice-over proclaimed a particular dealership to be the 'most premier' dealer of
the many area dealers offering such cars. Such usage can be heard all the time.
Are these English language speakers just being lazy, or do they have a problem
that runs a bit deeper? It may be that their language consists of sets of inflexible
scripts that are difficult to unglue. If 'you guys' is indelibly stuck together meaning 'any set of people not including me', then it would be difficult to separate
such a script when possession is the issue. If all things that deserve emphasis
begin with 'most', it would be difficult to drop the most when referring to something that is 'premier'.

Another such example came my way on a plane trip from St. Louis to Orlando. The steward offered the current weather conditions in Orlando, saying it
was 'ninety degrees and chances of showers'. Given two hours and ten minutes
to ponder the logic underlying this choice of words, I concluded that he must
have pluralized chance, as showers is a plural, giving us 'chances of showers'
rather than 'a chance of showers'. Before departure he'd told us we could leave
the plane as departure had been delayed, but we shouldn't 'straddle too far from
the aircraft'. Presumably he meant 'stray'.

Breaking Up Scripts

There is considerable evidence that the earliest kind of knowledge is the acquisition of scripts or *schemata*—defined as general knowledge frameworks about
typical events and conversations (Nelson, 1986). Developmental psychologists
propose that a child's acquisition of specific knowledge is built upon his current
state of internal schemata. If this is true, it may mean that children who continue

to think and speak in scripts are stuck, so to speak, at a holistic level of scripts, unable to develop on into the world of the specific.

If these children think and speak in scripts of words that get stuck together over the years like a broken record repeating the same sorry word pattern for much too broad a range of situations, it would seem a prudent instructional move to break these scripts up, teaching children to manipulate units of meaning into and out of phrases. Our *Language Wise* lesson Stand Ins is just for that purpose. In Stand Ins the child is offered a simple sentence and must replace one unit of meaning. So in the sentence, *The motorcycle is loud*, the child must replace 'loud'. Sometimes the child is told that the meaning must remain the same, and sometimes he's directed to change the meaning of the sentence when he changes the target word. Different units of meaning can be targeted to allow the child an opportunity to discover stand in words, and the relative importance of the various units of meaning to the overall thought. So in the above example, if the child is directed to change *loud* and keep the meaning the same he'll review his vocabulary for a word meaning the same as loud. He may come up with something like 'noisy'. If on the other hand he's asked to change the meaning by changing the word *is*, he may come up with *was*, or *will be*, making a discovery about the temporal relevance of these words as units of meaning in an overall thought. Stand Ins can be found on page 196, in section two.

I Think Therefore I Am

Why is it that one child becomes a word gymnast, playing adeptly with language, while another becomes inflexible and rigid, limited to scripts he has glued together over the years, sounding much like the proverbial 'broken record'? Could this inflexibility in language be prevented? It's tempting to think, "My child will never have this sort of problem because I don't speak this way, and he's in a good school where he hears proper word usage." But there is some evidence that what children hear is not the only issue. What children believe about language may be of equal importance. Meta-language acquisition—if you will allow this turn of phrase—may be a critical ingredient in language acquisition. How children think of words and word parts will determine the strategies they enlist in learning new words, and in learning how to form a sentence. If, as we suggested in the previous section, children learn scripts or clauses of meaning and never focus in on the smallest units of meaning, the morphemes of their language, they end up forming strained verse that hinges on surrounding words and clauses rather than the flexible language tactics of the verbally intelligent—the *language wise*. Your child's eventual flexibility will hinge on your ability to grease those language wheels now while he's young and his mind is ready, willing and able to spring from greater to smaller parts as needed to unlock meaning in words, phrases, sentences, chapters, and books.

Creating scenarios in which children are made aware of language—its structure, parts, and mechanics—is no easy task. In chapter three we played *Word Detective* and *Connections*. In *Word Detective* our goal was to offer children a strategy for finding out the meaning of a word they don't know. *Connections* is intended to cause children to look for the relatedness of words when that relatedness is not easily perceivable. Let's have a go at another *Language Wise* activity. This one is intended to make children more aware of the various kinds of words and the functions they provide. We call this lesson the *Caveman Game*. In this game children are told what we believe about the history of language. They're cast into the world of the caveman and asked to communicate with nouns only, then with nouns and verbs, then with nouns, verbs and modifiers. Only at the end are they allowed to add in articles, prepositions and conjunctions. By depriving children of the right to use these words in their stories, the lesson teaches the usefulness of such words. It's fun and the kids really enjoy it. Let's have a go at it here. Use the following lines to write a little story about what you did last night. Remember to use nouns only.

_____

_____

_____

_____

_____

_____

Wasn't that fun? It's amazing how much meaning can be conveyed when we talk about the 'stuff' in our world. Here's my tale of what I did last night. See if you get the story line.

Canada taxi seatbelt driver money pocket airport suitcases lady ticket passport monorail plane chair seatbelt laptop book lady food juice pillow neck back legs lady pillows seatbelt airport Florida passport suitcases husband daughter car seatbelt home suitcase dogs cats wine bed

You may have noticed while writing your story that you don't think in complete sentences and then take out everything else to do this activity. Its really quite easy to write in nouns only. After all, that stuff is what filled your evening, not the articles and prepositions. When you read my story you might have noticed that the actions are sort of implied by the relationship of the nouns. *lady food* for instance is pretty clear—lady <u>brought</u> food. How else could it have gotten there if no other player is mentioned? Food doesn't travel unassisted by a player. When you read this kind of story, you realize how verbs might have been imagined between nouns in man's early language. If thought is father to the word—if need determines language—it's no wonder verbs appeared in speech. The Caveman lesson can be found on page 210 , section two. Use it. Play with it. After this lesson was sent home for homework with an eight year old *Language Wise* student at Read America, his mom came in the next evening to pick him up after a lesson. "I used this technique to write a staff memo to my department today. They loved it! I think it might be the first memo they've actually read in years!" The contents of the memo are pictured here. Apparently Sue's staff had no trouble figuring out that they each needed to log in their vacation dates by Tuesday.

from the desk of Sue

paper pencil calendar vacation me desk Tuesday

Teaching Children to Anticipate Meaning

If independent units of meaning are critical to an overall complete thought, it would stand to reason that being able to anticipate units of meaning based on previous units of meaning, as the complete thought unfurls, would be a useful skill. We call this skill 'pacing'. Pacing assures that the spoken or written words are a perfect mirror reflection of what's happening in the world. Being good at pacing will prevent 'barking up the wrong tree'. Let's do one of these together. In the following example write down what you think might follow. Then turn the book upside down and read the next part of the passage. Change your answer accordingly.

The boy walked _____.

When he got there he went swimming.

The boy walked_____.

On the next line write a statement summarizing why your original end to the first phrase didn't work after you read the next phrase.

_____

_____

_____

Here's a real answer from a real *Language Wise* client. In fact, this answer came from Sue's son Jeremy, who is eight years old.

The boy walked <u>to the library</u>_____.
When he got there he went swimming.
             <u>to the beach</u>_____.
<u>You usually don't swim at the library. There isn't any water there except maybe</u>
<u>the sprinklers. You can play in the sprinklers, but you can't swim in them.</u>

Here's another answer offered by thirteen year old Chad.

The boy walked <u>his dog   </u>.

When he got there he went swimming.

<u>   to the swimming pool   </u>.

<u>When you walk your dog you don't actually 'get' anywhere, you just walk. So I</u>

<u>changed my answer to have the boy walk somewhere. If he's going to swim</u>

<u>when he gets there, it should be a pool that he walks to.   </u>

Elaborative Measures May be Needed

Another useful skill that will replace the old scripts with new pieces is elaboration. The skill of elaboration may be as old as the spoken word. In London's
Hyde Park there is a special spot called Speaker's Corner. This location has been
known for hundreds of years as a safe place for the disgruntled to go and speak
their mind. After hearing of this wonderful place, I set up a place in our home
where our daughter Mandy could have it out with whatever might be bothering
her about Mom and Dad's parenting techniques. It's very effective. At the north-
east corner of the house, where bedroom and bathroom meet, Mandy will say
things she wouldn't dream of saying elsewhere. This all came about after a recent tour of England, on which Mandy had not been invited. On my return
Mandy was sulky and quiet. When asked what the matter might be, her answer
was, "Nothing." Later that day, as her 'act' went on. I told her about Speaker's
Corner and invited her to pick a spot in the house for such a use. She immedi-
ately perked up, went over to the aforementioned spot and proceeded to tell me
why she felt she should have accompanied me on my trip to England. Though I
was sorely tempted, I never responded. Speaker's Corner is, after all, a safe
place—no criticisms, no recriminations, no defense, no punishment—just the
corner, the speaker, and whatever is on his mind. Twenty-five minutes later
Mandy stopped bleating and was a delight for the remainder of the weekend.
   Elaboration through filibustering has long been used as a means of persuasion through wearing down one's opposition. Written record of the filibuster
goes back to the Senate of ancient Rome. In a filibuster, one or more parties with
an argument to be made gain control of the floor and continue speaking on their
chosen topic until they believe the opposition is beginning to give way to the idea

they're forwarding. The intention is to block action until some persuasion has occurred, or until the session has ended with no action taken. The filibuster can be used for good or ill. The most notorious filibuster in US history occurred in 1964 when several senators filibustered against the Civil Rights Bill.

Infants and young children are extremely gifted in the art of filibuster, offering quite elaborate and creative arguments. Have you ever seen a two year old fussing for something he wants? His technique is to be envied—and usually it works. As children mature they often become less willing to talk incessantly about anything. Perhaps it's something we say to them like, "Sit down and be quiet." At any rate, the skill seems lost to most children by about age seven. The average seven or eight year old when asked, "What did you do at school today?" will respond with, "Nothing." Even field trips and visits from veterinarians with exotic species in tow will gain you a mildly interested response like, "Went on a field trip," or "A man with some animals came." The report pictured here was written by eight year old Robert. At the end of his kindergarten year Robert's teacher had referred him for I.Q. testing because he was being considered for the gifted program at his school. Her recommendation included the statement,

"Robert is very bright. He is outgoing and cooperative and shares many creative insights with the rest of the class. I highly recommend that he be tested for the first grade gifted class." Robert was tested. He missed the I.Q. cut off by two points. Robert wrote this piece one and a half years later in February of second grade. Notice that he just lists what he did and what he saw. The use of lists is very common in such assignments. It is equally common to see repetition such as, "It was fun."

Robert Cummings
Mrs. Simms
2/2/98

Our Class Field Trip

We went to the zoo. We saw animals. It was fun. We saw lions. We saw hipos. We saw baby birds. We ate lunch. We played on the toys in the petting zoo. We went back to schol. It was fun.

When we teach a child the art of elaboration, we begin with very narrow topics. This requires the child to stretch his way of thinking about the subject, and to use many words to talk about the subject. We begin with speech and then move on to written pieces. Let's try one below. This one is my favorite. The topic is an egg. It's best to have a specimen to ponder while you do this. Go ahead— write down everything you can think of to say about an egg. Don't limit yourself to one page. Have more paper handy.

The Egg

_____

_____

_____

_____

_____

_____

_____

_____

_____

_____

_____

_____

_____

_____

_____

_____

_____

_____

I think teachers sometimes make the mistake of assigning topics that are broad so that the child will have lots to write about. This invites lists, like those seen in Bobby's field trip report. It also invites one basic comment about many things rather than many thoughtful comments about one thing. Our elaboration lesson does the opposite. It forces the child to write a lot about one thing. Brinnae's dad (the lawyer mentioned previously) invented an activity that really helped Brinnae (age seventeen) become much more verbally inclined. You may recall that Brinnae did badly in high school and her dad feared she would not be able to make it into law school eventually. This activity was intended to improve her working vocabulary, and general verbal skills. He wrote down about thirty topics (like egg) and put them in a cookie jar. Each evening when he got home he would shake up the jar, open the lid and pass it to Brinnae. All this was going on while he cooked dinner. Mom is a crime reporter and works evenings until 11:00 P.M. Choosing a topic at random, Brinnae was expected to speak for a period of time on that topic. The time she was expected to speak started at five minutes and by the end of the first month she spoke for fifteen minutes on random topics. A few months later, when Brinnae shared this activity with her Speech 101 teacher at the community college she now attends, he liked the idea so much that he ended each class session by choosing one student to draw from a list of topics and elaborate for five minutes.

Elaboration can be taught in another way by playing the game *Guess What* in section two. Taking turns, one player chooses an object and offers a series of clues and the other guesses what the object is, based on the clues. I have a favorite one I reserve for the older kids. See if you can figure out what this is:

I am an animal.

I have no eyes.

I have a long tail.

I have a nice pad.

In hard times I keep on rolling.

I'm really wired up!

Although I'm a rodent, I have a shell like a turtle.

I do my business on your desk.

That last one is a dead give away! Of course it's a *computer mouse.*

A Lean, Mean Questioning Machine

Another developmental milestone is the appearance of questions in the child's language. Dale (1976) found that children learn to turn a statement into a question when the MLU reaches 2.5. What, where and who are the first questions that children ask, with when and why following in a few months (Bloom, Markin & Wootten, 1982). Why is yet another milestone. Why implies that the child understands causality. When why appears, it's very important to treat it with the respect it's due. It's very tempting to answer these onslaughts of questions with "Because" or "That's just the way it is." This is a dangerous path. The child who hears, "Because" as an answer to "Why is the sky blue?" will be the child who will answer his parent's question, "What did you do at school today?" with, "Nothing." Every question has an answer. I know it's hard when the questions are so frequent and quite frankly, so difficult! Why is the sky blue? Come on, does anyone know the answer to this? Carl Sagan probably did, but he died, having written hundreds of books, papers and speeches, none of which were geared to children. Why is the sky blue anyway? Well here are a few acceptable answers.

Air is blue when there's a lot of it.

All the colors are made when light shines on or through things. When light shines through air it makes the color blue.

There's a bunch of air clinging to our planet. When the sun shines on it, it looks light blue. When the clouds are out, it looks gray. At night it looks black.

Answers to this and other difficult questions needn't be textbook answers. They should be as true as you can muster given your knowledge of the facts. Your child needn't necessarily understand the entire answer you offer. What's important is that he does get an answer. It's a natural reflex of the brain to question. That reflex will die off in time if it receives no rewards.

Even worse than no answer is a sarcastic answer. This child will answer the,"What did you do at school today?" question with, "None of your business." I heard a child, who looked to be of kindergarten age, ask who I believe might have been his grandmother, this question, "Why are there seven days in weeks?" Her answer, "Because nobody could think of a name for another day." Well, I'm no expert on this stuff, but I know that's not true. Why would anybody lie to a child? Here are some more positive answers.

Our planet goes all the way around the sun one time each year. That's one time for every time you have a birthday. In a year there are 365 days. That seemed like a lot of days to try to remember, so someone probably thought it would be easier to re-member fewer days, over and over again, instead. People can remember seven things pretty well. You can remember the seven numbers in our phone number. And, you can remember all the days of the week too.

Here's my all time worst kid's question compliments of my son Rob, circa 1982. *"Why do some people be mean?"* My answer was brief and to the point. *"Some people are mean because they don't know how great it would be if everybody were nice."*

Some questions may require a delay until an answer can be offered. When our daughter Mandy was growing up, we kept a wipe off board in the laundry room just for her questions. If a question was too big for Mom or Dad, we wrote the question on the board and when we had time, we found the answer. This teaches children that answers are worth seeking.

I'm Learning What I Should Do to Help My Child's Language Development. What's the Responsibility of My Child's School?

If as we've suggested, children easily learn language that reflects the physical properties (things, actions and modifiers) of the world around them, and if as numerous studies indicate, the child acculturates the remaining words (articles, prepositions, conjunctions) that make up his language, it would stand to reason that parents and teachers could easily make a child *less* language wise by failing to expose him to certain turns of phrase. In a classic study, language researcher Roger Brown placed babies who were in the telegraphic stage of language devel-opment (two and three MLUs per sentence) in front of two television screens. On one screen Big Bird was tickling Cookie Monster. On the other screen Cookie

Monster was tickling Big Bird. A voice-over said, "Look at Big Bird Tickling Cookie Monster." These infants had no trouble with this fairly complex command. In another study (deVilliers, 1979) researchers asked children to point to the picture of "The boy was hit by the girl." The majority of children under six years of age indicated the picture of the boy hitting the girl. In commands that made no sense if the subject and object were reversed, such as, "The candy was eaten by the girl," the children indicated the correct picture. These studies beg some very important questions about educational practices.

Are We Expecting Too Little of Our Children?

Are we making our children *less* language wise by talking to them in very simple sentences? I think we may be. Even children's literature is being rewritten in progressively simplistic language. If you look at books written in the 1950s, books like *Encyclopedia Brown*, you see fairly complex sentence structure—sentences like, "It was with grave concern that Encyclopedia Brown answered the question," and "Despite his mother's warnings, Encyclopedia Brown left for school without his warm winter jacket." *Encyclopedia Brown* is just one example of thousands of children's stories with wonderfully complex sentences. *Winnie-The-Pooh* is one of our favorites. Pooh even stops to poke fun at 'big words'. This passage offers a wonderful opportunity for children to learn a few new words.

> *"The atmospheric conditions have been very unfavorable lately," said Owl.*
>
> *"The what?" asked Pooh.*
>
> *"It's been raining," offered Christopher Robin.*

We aren't alone in our concerns that children are being dumbed down by the instruction they get. Some other books with this theme include *Losing Our Language* by Sandra Stotsky, *Dumbing Down Our Kids* by Charles Sykes, *Dumbing Us Down* by John Taylor Gatto, and *Learning All the Time*, the last of ten books on education by John Holt.

Rich language and sentence structure require the reader to delay the leap to closure and wait until further into the sentence before meaning starts to unfold.

A survey of two hundred twelve children's books in print in 1998 found very little of this complex language. Many publishers of children's literature are even re-writing the classics with very simple language. Adults are subjected to dumbing down as well. We looked at newspapers from the last one hundred twenty years. Since the fifties there has been a sharp decline in both the length and the structural complexity of sentences appearing in the news. A random sampling of medium size city newspapers from 1890 to 1930 showed a mean sentence length (MSL) of thirty-seven words, compared to twenty-six words in 1998. Also revealing are the MLUs, weighing in at forty-five from 1890 to 1930 and thirty in 1998.

LENGTH OF SENTENCES IN NEWSPAPERS 1890-1998		
	1890-1930	1998
MSL	37	26
MLU	45	30

As we've mentioned, not just the length, but the structure of sentences has deteriorated. We pulled this sentence from the *Sanville Weekly News*. It ran just after the death of Robert Lincoln in 1926. *Mr. Lincoln has been accused of being a sort of hermit and was <u>very little seen</u> in public in later years, but this was because of his <u>abhorrence of things political,</u> and the fact that he was being <u>eternally pointed out as</u> "Abe Lincoln's son."* Notice the interesting turns of phrase we've underscored.

Dumbing down doesn't end with the newspaper. The professions and academic disciplines may be suffering as well. In a 1996 column, Dear Abby offered over a dozen quotations from actual court documents. The following is an example of real language spoken by real attorneys in real courtrooms.

Attorney: **"Mrs. Jones, do you believe you are emotionally stable?"**

Mrs. Jones: **"I used to be."**

Attorney: **"How many times have you committed suicide?"**

Apparently this attorney's language development didn't include details on the fatality of suicide. Presumably he meant, how many times had she *attempted* suicide? Are we splitting hairs—holding everyone to too high a standard? We think not. Presumably the mental stability of Mrs. Jones was of paramount importance to the outcome of the case being heard. In fact, Mrs. Jones could have answered the question with an honest, "Never." She was after all still alive.

Are today's simplistic sentences training children that they needn't do much work to gain meaning? Are we actually conditioning children to construct scripts glued together with holistic meanings attached—often wrong meanings? Is this training leaving them handicapped? In 1997 we were curious to find out if children could perform as well as deVilliers' subjects in 1979, who, by age five or six, could gain the appropriate meaning of object-first sentences like, "The boy was hit by the girl." We were stunned at what we found. We asked twenty-six children age six to fourteen (average age ten years, one month—all within normal verbal intelligence as measured by the Peabody Picture Vocabulary Test-r) to choose the correct picture for "The boy was hit by the girl." Only fifteen of these children indicated the correct picture. In addition we found no evidence that this was a developmental issue after age six. Some of the oldest children answered incorrectly and some of the youngest children answered correctly. Are the children of 1997 less able to understand a complex sentence than the children of 1979? Are we dumbing down our children? How else can we explain the apparent slide in the ability to comprehend the sentence? We also wanted to find out what children would come up with if asked open ended questions about complex sentences. We read the following sentence to each child in the above mentioned group individually: "While staring out the window I felt a great sadness." We asked them, "What does this mean?" Only ten of the twenty-six children offered a correct response. Thirteen said, "Staring out the window made the person sad." Three of the children said, "Staring out the window made you sad." These children assumed that the researcher reading the sentence was the "I" mentioned in the sentence.

We then asked the children, "What happened in this sentence?" and read, "Lifting his book bag out of the trunk, the boy told his mother all about his day at school." Nineteen out of twenty-six said something like, "The boy took his book bag out of the trunk." This response indicated that the children, grasping for one and only one bit of information about this passage, settled for the first bit, leaving out the important part that followed. If the child's answer included, "A boy told his mother about school," we gave credit for a correct answer.

When read the next sentence the children were asked to "Summarize this sentence"—"The girl sat upon the stool and thought of all the ways she had disappointed her parents this week." Nine of the twenty-six offered an acceptable answer. Eleven said, "The girl sat this week," six said, "The girl was being punished." The results of this mini-study are frightening. We've pictured them here on a graph showing the ratio of answers that were accurate and thorough, compared to answers that were wrong or omitted important elements of information.

COMPREHENSION OF COMPLEX SENTENCE STRUCTURE
twenty-six children age six to fourteen, average age ten years, one month.

PASSAGE	PARTIAL OR WRONG ANSWER	ACCURATE ANSWER
The boy was hit by the girl.		
While staring out the window I felt a great sadness.		
Lifting his book bag out of the trunk, the boy told his mother all about his day at school.		
The girl sat upon the stool and thought of all the ways she had disappointed her parents this week.		

Are We "Dumbing Down" Our Children in the Name of "Developmental Appropriateness"?

There has been a growing trend toward developmentally appropriate educational practices these past ten to fifteen years. This trend, though well intentioned and generally a good idea, carries some dangers. Before we can talk about 'developmental appropriateness' we must have a clear understanding of what is developmentally appropriate, and that understanding must be based in solid research. As you've seen from this book, a lot of research has been done on language development. We know a lot about what is appropriate at different ages. We're not sure that this information is always taken into account when the term 'developmentally appropriate' is used. We're equally unsure that the practices carried out in the name of developmental appropriateness are all developmentally appropriate. It seems to us that much time is spent on 'readiness' and not nearly enough on 'doingness'. Are some children being held back?

A young child learning to speak his native language is doing just that. He's not learning to speak baby talk. He should not be spoken down to. He should be offered the language as it is spoken. If he is spoken down to, when will he actually learn the language? Remember, from the work of Itard and others, there is a sensitive period for language development. We must offer children their language before they pass through the sensitive period for learning it. It's dangerous to wait around, speaking in four word sentences, while they are made ready for the good stuff. What exactly is going to happen to make them read? The absurdity of the notion that children should be spoken to in short basic sentences is illustrated in a study conducted by Shatz and Gelman in 1973. In this study, three to five year old children were asked to explain something in turn to a child of their own age, an older child and an adult. These children tailored their explanation to meet the age of the listener. These tiny little guys, just three to five years old, who we've offered four word sentences, are adjusting their speech to suit us! They're using developmentally appropriate practices on us! Maybe they don't really need our short sentences. Maybe we should offer up the full blown unabridged version of what's on our minds. Maybe publishers should stop dumbing down the next generation of book buyers.

Is Phonics "Dumbing Down" Our Children?

The predominant reading method for the past one hundred years has been Phonics. Phonics is a system of rules for teaching the various sounds that letters and sets of letters represent. Phonics exposes children to very basic text. Phonics takes about two to three years of instruction, with a success rate of about sixty-seven percent according to adult literacy scores of people educated during historical periods when Phonics has been used. Phonics relies on controlled text, such as the excerpt shown below, until second or third grade.

> See Spot run. Spot ran fast. Spot is sad. Spot did
> not get a bone. See Ned run. Ned ran fast. Ned
> is glad. Ned got a bone.

Sentences like the ones above are no joke. They're not an exaggeration of how very contrived basal readers are. This wouldn't be so worrying if reading instruction was occurring at the telegraphic stage of language development. But it isn't. It's occurring at five, six, seven and even eight years of age—at the cusp and past the sensitive period of language development! This wouldn't be much of an issue if Phonics worked fast enough for the process to end quickly and children could move on to literature, but it doesn't. Imagine being made to read passages like the above, daily for three years! Language being offered to a child should not be beneath his level. It should not be at his level. It should be just above his level—so he learns to view language as a fluid system of combining units of meaning in order to structure complete thoughts, rather than a series of brief scripts that he must memorize all in a row, like his address, or the spelling of his name.

Is Whole Language "Dumbing Down" Our Children?

Mixed in with Phonics instruction these past fifteen to twenty years has been Whole Language, the notion that children should focus on the meaning of text, seeking clues from many sources. Although Whole Language practices vary greatly from instructor to instructor, the original credos of the innovators directed teachers to have children focus on the words they can read, skipping difficult words, using pictures to gain meaning, skipping ahead when they don't understand something, and attempt to anticipate the story line. In short, Whole Language was based on the idea that meaning is everything. Like 'developmental appropriateness', this plan has backfired. As a follow-on to a 1996 (*Orton Annals of Dyslexia*) study conducted at the Read America clinic, children taught using Whole Language alone, or Whole Language in combination with Phonics were found to make frequent reading errors based on meaning seeking practices such as those mentioned above. These children tend not to notice their errors when reading, accepting any meaning that's remotely possible, with no concern for accuracy or consistency. The following example is taken from our last book, *Reading Reflex* (Free Press, 1998).

> Leroy got his car keys and walked out to the garage.

This passage was read by third grade Daniel as, "Larry got his care keys and went out to his garbage." This is not an isolated example. This is very common with children taught using Whole Language alone or in combination with Phonics.

While the innovators of Whole Language felt that the child should be allowed creativity in seeking meaning, they failed to consider whether meaning is a creative endeavor. Consider this—I tell eight year old Tommy that mammals are warm blooded animals who deliver live offspring. Should I expect or want Tommy to be creative with my words? I think not. What I want and expect is that Tommy understands my meaning—that's *my* meaning. I should think that Rudyard Kipling would feel much the same about *The Elephant's Child*. Creativity, which will be discussed in great detail in chapter six, is not part of understanding someone else's meaning. Creativity may follow understanding, and it's lovely if we can get the children to use it when they're committing words to paper or vocal cords, but it is not theirs to apply to meaning. Meaning is meaning—if we put it up for grabs, it's grabs we'll get. What we want instead of guesses and creativity, are self-discipline and precision.

What might parents and teachers learn from the practices of developmental appropriateness, Phonics, and Whole Language? If children are offered short, simple, structured sentences during the sensitive period of their language development don't be surprised if their language is limited to short, simply structured sentences. If children are offered very basic text for two to three years at the cusp of their sensitive period for language, don't be surprised if they speak and write in very basic sentences. If children are taught to guess to achieve meaning, don't be surprised that they guess and that their guesses are frequently wrong.

Are Vocabulary Programs in Line with the Way Children Learn Language?

Many vocabulary programs marketed to schools and teachers place a great deal of focus on *etymology*—the origin of words and word parts. Children are expected to know the discrete meanings of prefixes and suffixes as well as their etymologies. Is this valid? Is it in keeping with the way children learn language? As we saw from Berko's 'wug' experiment, five year olds surmised the meaning of 'wugs' from having been shown a picture of a single 'wug'. But, did these children explicitly know the meaning of 's' or was this information implicit? These children were told nothing about the origin of the word 'wug'. This is an important consideration to teachers and schools considering spending valuable instructional hours on teaching the meanings of prefixes and suffixes and the etymologies of these and the root words they're affixed to. Clearly we sometimes can determine the meaning of a new word by reaching inside for a root word that we already know. But is this a foolproof strategy that children can rely on? And do they use it? We must ask ourselves this before we set up strategies that will fail children, leaving them doubting the reliability of the next thing we teach them. On a recent school tour we observed a class of eight year old children working on their vocabulary lesson. The veteran teacher had written the word 'sanitation' on the board. Next to it she wrote the word 'sanitary'. She explained that 'sanitary' is the root word for 'sani<u>tion</u>' (underlining *tion*) and that 'tion' was a Latin suffix that made the root word into a noun. After some consideration a freckle faced red headed boy raised his hand and said quite sensibly, "Why isn't it 'sanitary-tion'?" The teacher answered to say that sometimes we just use *part* of the root word to make the new word, and she underlined part of the word (<u>sani</u>tary), explaining that this was the root. Now a girl in the front row furrowed her brow and said, "So why isn't it 'sani-tion'?" The teacher cleared her throat, laughed nervously and explained that we use certain letters to connect up the root and the suffix. Promising more on that tomorrow, she asked the children to take out their journals and write a few words on their plans for the weekend. A few minutes later the red headed boy raised his hand and announced proudly to the class, "I'm going to Sanibel Island this weekend... 'sani, sani!'," he echoed. The teacher commented that that was very nice and maybe he could bring back some seashells to share with the other children. This teacher's lesson is a clear example of everything going wrong. She certainly had her <u>sani</u>ty tested that day.

The issues here are numerous! Children (and adults) don't process language in bits of words. The original Latin 'sani' had meaning to the Romans. To us it's just part of a word—words like *sanitary, sanitation, Sanibel Island*, and *sanity*. In English we *defrock* a minister, but we don't *depose* a model or *depress* a drycleaner. We don't *defeat* or even *defeet* a podiatrist. If we do hear of a model being *deposed* or a drycleaner being *depressed*, we gather a very different meaning altogether—and not because we happen to know that the Latin root for the 'press' in depress is from the premier Latin root word 'depressus' meaning to 'press down'. Our brains simply don't go in that di<u>rec</u>tion when we encounter a new word. How about that 'rec' in 'direction'? What's that about? A peek in the dictionary will tell us that it's the English derivation of 'regere', Latin for 'align'. Of course a peek will also tell us the *meaning* of 'direction'—which is what we *really* want to know.

Other Fun Words

despite	when a gossip columnist loses her column
detract	when a farmer loses his farm
design	when a sign maker loses his sign company
denude	when a Playboy model loses her modeling rights
define	when a traffic court judge is removed from the bench
detour	when a vacationer goes back to work
detest	when a university is closed for spring break

The steps involved in the process of learning a new word are largely implicit. They involve inference and analogy. These skills are very different indeed from those typically taught in vocabulary development. The ability to use inference and analogy in vocabulary development necessitates the ability to use inference and analogy. So let's teach that!

How Many Words is a Lot?

We opened this chapter with the one year old using his first words. By age five he knows five to ten thousand words. By age six he knows eight to fourteen thousand words, and will learn two hundred-fifty new words in first grade. He will also have learned how to restructure his message if he gets a blank stare from his listener (Flavel, 1985). In second and third grades he'll learn five hundred new words each year, and in fourth grade he'll learn another two thousand two hundred fifty new words. In fifth grade and sixth grades these highs begin to decline and he will learn only sixteen hundred new words (Chicago & Minneapolis Public Schools, 1995).

Is twelve to eighteen thousand words enough to finish up sixth grade? It seems like a lot, but look at the differential—six thousand words! That means that children who are in the same class with kids who know twelve thousand words by sixth grade are trying to get by knowing six thousand fewer words than

their classmates. In the next chapter we'll take a close look at memory and attention to see what additional tools parents and teachers can use to move their
children and students to the high end of this chart.

GROWTH IN VOCABULARY ACROSS THE GRADES

Age 5	5,000 - 10,000 words
Age 6	8,000 - 14,000 words
Age 7	8,500 - 14,500 words
Age 8	9,000 - 15,000 words
Age 9	11,250 - 17,250 words
Age 10	12,850 - 18,850 words

CHAPTER FIVE

REMEMBERING

ATTENTION AND MEMORY IN LEARNING

In this chapter you will learn

The various kinds of attention that affect your child's verbal intelligence.

How information makes its way through levels of memory for later recall, and how you can positively affect the outcome.

The part that memory plays in comprehension.

How to help your child commit information to long term memory.

What an *orienting task* is and how you can use orienting tasks as a powerful instructional tool when you work with a child.

How to present information to your child based on the type of information it is.

About implicit and explicit learning and when to encourage each.

When our daughter Mandy was in the fifth grade her teacher spent the entire year teaching the Renaissance. At the end of summer we went to the open house hosted by the middle school Mandy was to transfer into. Dutifully we moved from class to class simulating what were to be Mandy's movements around the school each day. In each class we met another enthusiastic teacher who told of his or her plan for keeping the kids on track as they made the important transition into secondary education. When we got to her modern world history class we were told that they would begin at the Renaissance. We looked at each other both thinking the same thing, "This is a waste of her time. She already knows all about the Renaissance." When we'd completed our progression we went off to dinner together. Making her way to the bottom of a chocolate shake Mandy looked up and said, "How are we going to get all the way from the tenth century to the twentieth century in one school year?" I think of that night as the 'milkshake inquisition', a second round of chocolate shakes was ordered and Dad began to probe. By the third shake it was pretty clear that Mandy had spent the summer forgetting everything Mrs. Chalone had taught her about the Renaissance. Most parents have had a similar awakening of some kind. It's very frightening to be faced with the possibility that your child can't recall anything she's taught.

Imagine what your life would be like if you couldn't recall previous experiences. Every event, every experience, every word would be a novel one. You wouldn't learn from your experiences; they would just keep repeating themselves, over and over again. Learning something as basic as not to touch a hot object would be impossible. You would just rediscover the meaning of *hot* with each new burn. We take our memory for granted in our experiences, collecting memories like so many old friends. Memory is a basic and precious part of learning language and anything else. It offers us success without having to repeat our errors to find the right answer. Instead we recall the errors and move right to success. Before memory can occur, attention must be engaged to some degree. Let's look at the part of attention and memory in learning and in particular in the development of verbal intelligence—what memory researchers call *semantic memory*.

Attention

Human beings move through life in various degrees of consciousness. How tuned in you are at any given moment will affect how much you recall of the events around you, what you hear and see. It is possible to learn much from very little attention to the moment, but this kind of *latent learning* requires lots and lots of repetition. We'll consider this in greater detail later in this chapter. Generally speaking, the higher the level of awareness or attention to the task, the greater the degree of learning or remembering of the detail of the information. Getting attention is not that difficult. It's holding attention that presents the challenge. Cognitive psychologist Albert Bandura said that attention "involves self-directed exploration of the environment and construction of meaningful perceptions." Margaret Matlin defines attention as "a concentration of mental activity." Under these definitions attention is an interaction between the learner and the environment. The child's environment includes physical stimulus, information, other children or siblings, teachers or parents. Given this it would seem that breakdown in the process of attention may occur in the environment as well as in the learner himself. Why then does education consider only the part of the learner in diagnosing attention problems?

Attention Deficit Disorder

The most common educational measure of attention is *Conner's Inventory*. It's a set of survey questions that must be answered about the learner. It's typically given to a teacher, a parent and one other significant adult who interacts with the child on a regular basis. The test does not actually measure the child's behavior. Instead it asks these adults to make the measurements—subjectively. Not one question on the survey asks for a judgment about the child's environment—the other half of the attentional process. When the three surveys have been analyzed and the child is found to have symptoms of attentional disorder, certain recommendations are made. Almost invariably these deal with the environment—"seat the child where he has fewer interruptions, give the child immediate feedback to questions, always give clear directions, assign one task at a time." We act as if these are odd arrangements for a child, made specially because of his attentional problems. But what child *wouldn't* benefit from these improvements to his environment? All children deserve the courtesy of these considerations.

And what of the information offered to the child? What form does it take? Does it require attention as defined by Bandura and other learning theorists— *self-directed exploration of the environment and construction of meaningful perceptions*? Or do schools and teachers just expect children to remember verbatim, artfully reciting factoids? Certainly all teachers have the right motives for their lessons, but where is the analysis of their success or failure? Is there any such analysis or is the entire burden laid upon the child's slim shoulders?

Kinds of Attention

Some cognitive psychologists theorize that there is not one single kind of attention, but at least two different kinds of attention. Walter Schneider and Richard Shiffrin have proposed two levels of processing relevant to attention. *Automatic processing* can be applied to highly familiar material or events, while *controlled processing* is necessary for difficult tasks and tasks involving unfamiliar material. In a 1977 study conducted by Schneider and Shiffrin, these researchers discovered that automatic processing is parallel (you can handle more than one item at a time), while controlled processing is serial (only one item can be attended to at a time). The instructional ramifications of this are huge. The scenarios speak for themselves. To a child who is not as naturally intelligent as his classmate, most information offered in class will be difficult and new. This child needs to be able to do controlled processing most of the day. In contrast his brighter classmate rarely encounters new or difficult information in class. This allows him to spend his days in automatic processing mode. The result is that he actually becomes unused to and unpracticed at controlled processing. When he does encounter something new or difficult, he is unable to manage it. In this way, both children are dumbed down by the system.

It could be said that attention is an intricate process of giving one's consciousness to a stimulus for a period long enough to notice and understand it. What environmental conditions encourage a child to notice and understand new information? These conditions apply.

1. NEW INFORMATION SHOULD BE JUST ABOVE THE CHILD'S CURRENT LEVEL OF EXPERTISE. IN THIS WAY IT INTERESTS HIM BECAUSE IT IS NOVEL, BUT IT ISN'T SO NOVEL AS TO BE UNHEARD OF, HAVING LITTLE OR NOTHING TO DO WITH HIS PREVIOUS KNOWLEDGE AND EXPERIENCES.

So if you're teaching the Renaissance, for instance, which is just above the child's intellectual expertise, you might include lots of discussion of lifestyles during the era so as to link it to his knowledge and experiences in his own life.

2. NEW INFORMATION SHOULD BE MADE RELEVANT TO THE CHILD, LINKED THROUGH ANALOGY TO HIS SPHERE OF EXPERIENCE AND CURRENT KNOWLEDGE.

Such an investigation of the Renaissance might include an outline of the child's lifestyle as compared to the lifestyle of a child during the Renaissance. Subtopics might be—*my house, my education, my hobbies, my food, my friends, my clothes.*

3. WHEN RECEIVING NEW INFORMATION THE LEARNER SHOULD HAVE BEEN GIVEN A FRAMEWORK OF EXPECTATIONS ABOUT THE NEW INFORMATION SO THAT HE IS MAKING JUDGMENTS ALONG THE WAY BASED ON HIS EXPECTATIONS.

Our student could have down a time line of when the Renaissance occurred in history, so as to ground it in temporal reference.

Beyond noticing and understanding we might hope for another moment or two in which to begin to integrate this stimulus into the learner's greater scheme of things for later recall—in other words we hope that some *learning* will occur. How much learning occurs depends on other processes still. Let's turn to memory for a broader picture.

Levels of Memory

Information can be committed to at least three levels of memory. In this section we'll explore these.

Sensory Store

The first thing that hits our consciousness comes through our senses—what we hear, see, feel, taste and smell. These are very powerful windows into the conscious mind. Even in sleep we process much of what goes on around us. Rising easily enough to an alarm clock, a cold draft, a baby crying, the smell of smoke, sunlight on our faces. Though powerful at getting our attention, the senses are not a good place to leave memories for long term care. This part of memory is called the sensory store. It's just the tip of the iceberg as far as memory is concerned. Once attention is gotten, the senses are only useful as a kind of recording device that allows us to play back the information in storage. Recalling a phone number exemplifies this perfectly. You bump into a business contact in the grocery store. He tells you to call him regarding *the big deal*. He hasn't got a business card on him and you haven't got a pen on you. "Have your people call my people regarding *the big deal* at 298-7016," he says as he dashes off. What do you do? If you're like most of us mere mortals you repeat the number to yourself over and over again until you can get to a pen and jot it down on the back of your hand or your forearm. This repetition is like a link between the original (him saying the number) and the facsimile (you writing the number). If interrupted, for instance by your eleven year old son saying, "Daddy, Daddy, can I have a candy bar?" the link can be irrevocably broken, lost forever to the wind.

Some people use more elaborate procedures still. Mixed strategies can reduce the memory load to the auditory or *echoic* system and the visual or *iconic* system. Some people employ a mixed strategy to recall phone numbers, committing for instance the first three numbers to visual memory and the last four to echoic memory. In this way neither system is overburdened with the full seven numbers. The two systems are completely independent of one another so the overall seven never becomes a problem. Each system deals independently with the task of recalling only what you committed to that system.

I had a friend in high school who could remember any phone number tactilely. She assigned all of her fingers a number from zero to nine starting with her left pinky and moving in order to her right pinky. When someone told her their phone number she would hold out her hands and say the number as she looked at the corresponding finger.

We used to live in a small city with about six telephone exchanges that were based on the part of town in which you lived. It was easy enough to recall a number by remembering where the number originated and the last four digits. Of course this technique depended on one knowing *by heart* the six exchanges and which part of town each was associated with.

What does it mean to know something *by heart*? This common term typically implies effortless knowledge, information that one knows so well, one needn't work at it any longer. How does one come to know something by heart? Is it simply a matter of running the recording long enough that the information is permanently stored? Or is active use of the information required? Let's have a look at how information makes its way from sensory store to short term memory, and then on to long term memory.

Short Term Memory Store

As I write I have particular knowledge that is important to me at the moment but won't be important later on—the whereabouts of other members of my household for instance. Husband Geoff and father-in-law Brian are on the golf course, daughter Mandy is reading in her bedroom, Fiona who is visiting from England is at the clinic observing sessions. These things are important to me right now, but next week I'll have no need to remember where everyone was at 2:47 pm last

Thursday. Also relevant right now is Geoff's request that I call and make a dinner reservation at Ivy's. If I forget this I'll get stuck cooking. I must also remember that at 4:45 I need to leave to pick up Sophie, who's at the vet getting her annual shots and grooming. Will I need to remember any of this beyond today? Probably not. These arbitrary bits of information are what fill our short term memories. Humans are very good at getting information into and out of short term memory storage. Age and the strategies one employs seem to have a dramatic effect on the outcome.

The rehearsal technique mentioned earlier appears to be a natural human strategy which appears in childhood and improves with age. In a study conducted by John Flavell in 1966, ten percent of five year olds in the study used rehearsal as a memory aid while sixty percent of the seven year olds did and eight-five percent of the ten year olds did. Some people are better at this than others. The strategy one employs can improve the rate of success. In a 1969 study Moely et al. presented children of varying ages with a series of pictures to remember. The pictures were drawn from categories, such as plants, animals, furniture, etc. Only the oldest group of children (eleven year olds) showed evidence of clustering the items according to their categories. This suggests that the tendency to organize and commit information to memory according to categories develops later than the tendency to rehearse information. However, this doesn't make sense according to what we know about the ability of children to categorize—a skill which, as we discussed in earlier chapters, develops very early in childhood. Other studies shed further light on this. In a 1986 study (Schneider) researchers used lists of words that varied in the degree to which they could easily be categorized. In this study, even very young children organized easily categorizable lists according to categories. This study tends to suggest that the ease of categorizability of the information affects the likelihood of this strategy being used in accordance with the age of the child. Another study sheds further light on this. Worden (1975) asked children as young as five to sort items according to categories. He then employed a recall test of the items. Even the five year olds used the categories as an aid to recall. A 1978 study conducted by Ceci and Howe presented children of four, seven and ten with a series of pictures that could be sorted in terms of categories such as animals, or themes, such as a western. The children were taught to sort the pictures according to both theme and category. The children then took a recall test employing cued questioning relating to the categories and themes, for instance, "Name all the western things." There was no performance difference between the age groups. A control group asked to recall the same items without the advance sorting activity showed a dramatic performance difference between the age groups, with four year olds performing poorly in comparison to seven year olds, and ten year olds significantly outperforming both groups. These last two studies tend to imply that young children simply aren't aware of the effect of categorizing on memory and therefore don't tend to employ this technique spontaneously, though they can be easily taught to do so. It follows that the more connections one can draw between apparently disparate and arbitrary bits, the more categories into which one can place these seemingly arbitrary bits, the greater the ability to relate and recall them.

Some information that goes into short term memory storage needs to make its way to long term memory storage. When your sixteen year old reads a chapter of his history book you hope that he'll recall enough about World War II to pass the test next Wednesday, but you also hope that at thirty-five he'll recall who the good guys were and who the bad guys were—and other relevant information. But short term memories are just that: *short term*. If not committed to long term memory storage they decay in time or are displaced by new memories (Waughn & Norman, 1965). How does such information make its way from short to long term memory storage? How can we assure that our children are actually learning, and not just getting through the test?

Comprehension and Memory

Educators place a great deal of emphasis on *comprehension*. What exactly does this mean? The dictionary defines comprehension as *understanding*. Okay, that's fair. Teachers hope that children will understand what they hear, experience and read. But are they expected to recall the information beyond the initial understanding and maybe a test administered shortly afterward? Are they expected to use the information, to integrate it with other information, to make judgments about it, to make assumptions about other information based on it, and to test those assumptions? Certainly parents and educators hope for these sorts of higher level functions, but is there some plan to bring this to fruition, or do parents and educators believe that intelligent, motivated students will do these things and less intelligent, less motivated students will not? Do parents and educators even know that they have a part in the outcome? Do they understand the different processes at work when a student is expected to *understand* for short term recall on a test versus *knowing* something? In a 1980 study Daneman and

Carpenter tested children on standard short term memory tests and standard reading comprehension tests used for educational testing. There was a high correlation between the scores on these two kinds of tests, indicating that what we measure when we measure comprehension is little more than short term memory—what Daneman and Carpenter called *working memory span*.

Working Memory Span

Working memory span is quantitative in nature. It refers simply to the amount of information that one can hold in near literal memory for a brief time while it is *worked* with. As you read this chapter for instance, you have a literal or nearly literal memory of what you've just read. Some people have more or less of this, but it's pretty standardly a couple of sentences, and it would be considered an anomaly to be able to retell, verbatim, more than three. So if you were to close the book right now you would be able to retell with pretty good accuracy what the last two to three sentences said almost word for word. The information before that would not be available word for word, but you would be able to tell what it was about, to *conceptualize* it. Try this right now with this paragraph.

Assuming you're a smart parent or teacher, you were probably able to retell pretty much word for word the last couple of sentences, and then tell the gist of the preceding sentences in the paragraph. You have conceptualized them, and in this way committed them to long term memory. If you hadn't conceptualized them you would recall nothing of them. They'd be lost to you for eternity. Information in working memory must make its way into long term memory or it will be lost, written over by the next thing to come along.

Long Term Memory Store

The distinction between short and long term memory is more than just quantitative. It is qualitative as well. Information committed to long term memory is not just recalled, it is *known*. Whereas short term memory requires work, long term memories are effortless. The information becomes part of our *schema*, part of our larger structure of information on this and related topics. I think of it as the difference between carrying around a block as opposed to placing the block into an existing wall of information. Just as you can't arbitrarily place a block addition onto a house, you can't place a new bit of information arbitrarily. It must fit with the larger scheme of things. It must make sense. In order to make sense, information must be categorizable—we must be able to organize it into other information that we already have. So in our example of learning the Renaissance for instance, we built on what is relevant and known to the child—*my house, my education, my hobbies, my food, my friends, my clothes*—to teach him about these things in relation to the Renaissance period of history, giving him a contextual picture of life in that period. It follows that the better the learner is at making connections between seemingly arbitrary factoids, the better able he will be to fit these into his existing overall schema. This kind of fluid thinking allows the learner to examine a new bit of information, scan existing knowledge and find a category in which to place the new information, committing it firmly to long term memory—Queen Elizabeth; *ruler, government, laws, etc.* The next level of this process is the making of creative analogies—the learner knows things about previously known X that allow him to make assumptions about newly learned Z. And the next level is to test these assumptions. These last two levels will be discussed in the next chapter in the context of *logical reasoning* and *creativity*. For the purposes of this chapter we'll examine in more detail how things go right or wrong in the formation of long term memories.

Receptive and Expressive Memory

It's important to understand that there are two ways of retrieving memories. *Receptive memory* is when you hear or see something and recall having heard or seen it before—recognition. *Expressive memory* is when you're actually required to express the thing you heard or saw. Receptive memory is easier as it is more *passive*, requiring *yes* and *no* kinds of answers. "Yes I've seen that man before, or heard that song." Expressive memory is more difficult as it is more *active*, "I know the song, and can tell you all the words." The implications for education are obvious. We'd like our children to have not only receptive memories of educational content, but expressive memories as well. As a more active process, expressive memory requires action upon the content one wishes to commit to long term expressive memory. Active use of material renders it more accessible expressively.

How Can I Help My Child Commit Information to Memory?

There is much that parents and teachers can do to establish good strategies for committing information to long term memory. Decades of research tell us everything we need to know to help our children and students become efficient learners. In this section we'll explore these with an eye toward integrating them into our daily interactions with our children and students.

Orienting Tasks

There is considerable evidence that the degree to which the learner is engaged in the task to be recalled will affect the success of long term learning. In chapter two we mentioned the *orienting task*. The orienting task gets the learner's attention and focuses him on the information to be learned. The orienting task seems to be a critical component to memory—a first cause if you will—engaging attention and personalizing it. Its unique quality is that it causes the learner to make a decision about the information, shifting the burden to the learner. By requiring a decision, it also requires interaction between the new information and old information—what the learner already knows, his existing *schema*. It's the first effort to make a place for the new information within the learner's existing cognitive structure.

In a series of experiments in 1975 (Craik and Tulving) and 1977 (Craik) researchers found that the type of orienting task required of the learner greatly affects the quantity and quality of long term memories associated with the task. In other words there is more than one way to get someone's attention, and these ways vary in their effectiveness. It stands to reason that the nature of the information being processed should be considered in designing orienting tasks. If you are attempting to engage the learner in a history lecture it would make sense to ask a question about what the causes of the historical events might be, since by its nature, historical study deals in causes and effects and the long term trends of these.

Subjectivity

Another important element of the orienting task is that the answer must be allowed to contain some degree of subjectivity. Warrington and Ackroyd (1975) studied the effects of the amount of subjectivity allowed in an answer on the quality of memories. They split their subjects into three groups. All three groups were shown pictures of faces. The first group was asked to judge each face as pleasant or unpleasant. The second group was asked to decide whether each face was long or short. The third group was the control group. They were asked to just try to recall each of the faces. Subjects were then shown another set of face pictures which contained a mix of some of the faces in the first trial and some new faces. They were asked to decide which faces they had seen in the first trial. The greatest recall came from the group who was asked to judge the faces for pleasantness or unpleasantness—the task which required subjective consideration. The group who was asked to determine whether the faces were long or short performed only slightly better than the control group, who was asked only to try to remember the faces. This particular kind of orienting task is called a *semantic orienting task*. It requires the use of concepts rather than just dimensions as in the second group's question regarding whether the faces were long or short. In a semantic orienting task the learner is required to call upon previously conceptualized information in making a judgment about the new information.

In conducting these studies Craik and Tulving noticed that semantic orienting tasks took longer than non-semantic orienting tasks which dealt only with dimension. They wanted to be certain that it was the task itself that improved the memory of their subjects and not just the longer time on task at processing the information. To test this they devised a non-semantic task that took longer to perform than the semantic task and compared memory in both cases. With a processing time of over twice as long as the semantic orienting task, the subjects in the non-semantic group still performed very poorly in comparison, showing that it is the subjective nature of the task rather than the time on task that makes semantic orienting tasks so powerful at improving memory.

A word of caution is in order here. Not all new material that a parent or teacher has to present to a child is up for subjective analysis. Clearly some things simply *are* what they *are*. A good rule of thumb is to use orienting questions a lot and to design them as *semantic orienting questions* whenever the material warrants subjectivity.

Getting good at requiring semantic orienting tasks of children takes time and energy on the part of parents and teachers. Some parents and teachers do this naturally without really knowing why. They are just more gifted than their neighbors at engaging children. Often these gifted folks are drawn to the field of education and the results are favorable. But this is not always the case, and it is always preferable to know why what you do works, so you can do more of it. In the following exercise we'll give you several scenarios in which to develop an orienting question. This will help you begin to think about how to cause a child to become engaged in various tasks. Remember that orienting questions should require the child to make a subjective judgment about the information. Take as long as you'd like to consider these. Discuss your ideas with your spouse, or other educators if you're a teacher. When you've come up with some answers turn the page for our suggestions in these scenarios. Our suggestions aren't the only correct answers. They're just some ideas about engaging a child in these scenarios.

Scenario One—Your eleven year old is rotten about doing chores. He seems willing, nodding his head and promising to get right on it, but somehow it never happens. It's Tuesday afternoon and you'd like him to get the trash out for the Wednesday morning pick up. Write down your orienting question.

_____

_____

_____

_____

Scenario Two—You're a teacher of eight year old children. You're lecturing on the topic of the Age of Exploration. You'd like the children to understand and remember what started this era. Write down your orienting question.

_____

_____

_____

_____

Scenario Three—You're explaining to your seven year old why she shouldn't be so mean to her little brother who has just turned six. Write down your orienting question._____

_____

_____

_____

Scenario Four—You're a sixth grade science teacher. You've always been fascinated by weather and never quite understood why eleven year olds don't seem to share your awe. Your students never do as well in your meteorology unit as you would like them to. Write down your orienting question.

_____

_____

_____

_____

Each suggestion is only one possible orienting question for these scenarios.

Scenario One—Your eleven year old is rotten about doing chores. He seems willing, nodding his head and promising to get right on it, but somehow it never happens. It's Tuesday afternoon and you'd like him to get the trash out for the Wednesday morning pick up.

"Oh Bobby, it's Tuesday. There is something I'm supposed to remember to do on Tuesdays. What is it? I can't remember, can you?"

Scenario Two—You're a teacher of eight year old children. You're lecturing on the topic of the Age of Exploration. You'd like the children to understand and remember what started this era.

"If you lived in a house with twenty other people and there wasn't enough room for you all, and food for everyone to eat, what would you do? Write down your ideas on a piece of paper."

Scenario Three—You're explaining to your seven year old why she shouldn't be so mean to her little brother who has just turned six.

"Maybe you should make up the rules for our house. We'll all do just what your rules say, so be careful to think of everything. I'll write them down for you. Ready when you are."

Scenario Four—You're a sixth grade science teacher. You've always been fascinated by weather and never quite understood why eleven year olds don't seem to share your awe. Your students never do as well in your meteorology unit as you would like them to.

"Everyone take out a piece of paper and draw a line down the middle. Now at the top of one side write Good Things About Rain and on the top of the other side write Bad Things About Rain. Make a list of as many things as you can think of."

Engaging the Whole Group

If you're working with a whole class or even small groups of children it's important that each of them is engaged through the orienting task. When you stand in front of a group of children and ask the group an orienting question one or two children will always be first to think of a response. The rest of the group isn't engaged if they haven't had to make a judgment about the information. By inviting the children to write down their answers you're engaging everyone. I use an *answer pail* for this when I work in groups of children. I have a plastic sand pail with a question mark drawn in permanent marker. I pass it for the children to deposit their answers. In this way each child has made a judgment. I draw from the pail rather than calling on children with raised hands. This also holds down the movement and noise level in the class.

If you're a parent with more than one child to engage you might try an idea box. A standard issue suggestion box on the kitchen counter will involve everyone in decisions, thereby exposing all parties to the orienting questions you devise.

Coordinality Assumption

Researchers Craik and Lockhart (1972) isolated another variable that plays an important part in the success of verbal intelligence instruction. They performed numerous experiments that showed that the nature of the processing of new information must match the nature of the information itself in order to be highly successful. So if for instance you're giving a lesson on reading the word *Table* to six year old children and the word happens to be capitalized, and should you begin your lesson with mention of the fact that the word is capitalized, you've oriented the children toward orthographic or *visual* stimuli rather than phonological or the *sounds* the letters represent. In this particular example it would be better to focus first on the sounds of the letters with questions like "What's the first sound?" and then discuss the capitalization after the fact, as an additional lesson.

Understanding the nature of the material you teach to children is straightforward enough and can be easily incorporated into the thought that goes into our lessons as teachers and parents. Before you begin working with your child on a task be well aware of what it is you are actually teaching him. If the task at hand is to teach him to find answers to questions embedded in the story, do not spend instructional time trying to get him to read with intonation. A more useful endeavor would be to teach him to listen for answers as he reads. If you're trying to teach him to write more meaningful sentences, do not spend instructional time teaching him to combine two boring sentences. A more useful task would be to teach him to add information to his existing sentences.

Associative Priming

Memory researcher Alan Parkin explored the effects of causing the learner to organize according to categories of memory. Parkin called this *associative priming*.
This is taught explicitly in our *Language Wise* activity *Operating on Memory*. In
this lesson the child is asked to take a list of words and sort them into sets that go
together, for recall later. Let's try this now. Here is a list of words. You organize
them into sets on the lines below the words.

> *cats, rainbow, ribbon, hippo, thermometer, hamster,*
> *water, leash, hair dryer, heat, shampoo, dog food*

_____	_____	_____
_____	_____	_____
_____	_____	_____
_____	_____	_____
_____	_____	_____

Now cover the top of the page and write down as many of the words as you can
think of here. *No peeking!*

_____	_____	_____
_____	_____	_____
_____	_____	_____
_____	_____	_____
_____	_____	_____

The list is easily organized into three categories; things that have to do with
weather; animals or things that have to do with animals; things that women use
to fix their hair. So you end up with this.

cats	rainbow	ribbon
hippo	thermometer	hair dryer
hamster	water	shampoo
leash	heat	_____
dog food	_____	_____

Or this. It doesn't matter how the categories are organized as long as they make sense to you.

cats	rainbow	ribbon
hippo	thermometer	hair dryer
hamster	_____	shampoo
leash	_____	water
dog food	_____	heat

Now remembering is chunked into the three short categories of related items rather than a long list of unrelated items. As we mentioned earlier in this chapter and in previous chapters, children are quite capable and very good at sorting and categorizing from a very early age. That doesn't necessarily mean that they realize the value of organizing information as a memory aid. This lesson is intended to teach them this strategy explicitly. Later today after you've read a bit more and maybe had a little snack, try it again here and see how many you can recall.

Elaboration Effect

As French novelist and author of *Remembrance of Things Past* Marcel Proust said, "We soon forget what we have not deeply thought about." One way to help our children and students retain what they understand is to cause them to consider deeply those things. Elaboration is an art nearly forgotten in this age of factoids and brief encounters of every kind. What did your son or daughter do last night after dinner? One hundred ninety million Americans watched a sitcom last night after dinner. I'm not greatly opposed to television watching. Our family does their share of it. But in sitcoms and television dramas problems are solved in the space of thirty to sixty minutes with no decision making on the part of the viewer. Unlike a book, it all happens so quickly that one hasn't got much of an opportunity to consider the possibilities. Watching television won't hurt your child; it's all the things he doesn't do that will hurt him. We must make our children, as

Proust says, *think deeply about things* if we expect them to remember them. Sitting in the laundry room and pondering the concept of an overfull trash can for later discussion may help Bobby remember to empty it the next time he notices that it's overfull. Another slightly less mean idea employs the television. Try watching a video just to the point before the climax of the story. Stop the video and have a family discussion about what might happen. You could take turns telling your version of the end. You could all tell a small piece and then pass it on for the next person to take up the tale, or you could all write down your own personal ending. Then turn the movie back on.

In a series of experiments conducted by Craik and Tulving in 1975 these psychologists found that elaboration improves memory for intricate material. In particular, setting up increased numbers of associations with new material was found to correlate very highly with lasting memory of new material. The researchers concluded that these increased associations caused a "more richly elaborated memory trace than simple categorization of the material." Our lessons *Elaboration* and *Connections*, both already described in earlier chapters, are excellent for this purpose.

Congruency Effect

Another phenomenon of interest to parents and teachers presenting new material to children is the *congruency effect*. It has been noted by numerous memory researchers that questions that evoke 'yes' answers are more memorable than questions that evoke 'no' answers. It could be assumed that 'yes' answers are more likely to be part of a coherent structure of thought associated with the material than 'no' answers—they flow, they follow a logical pattern toward the answer.

If taken to heart by educators, this would make true and false tests obsolete. It wouldn't make sense to write all the test items for only 'true' answers. Nor would it make sense to design 'false' questions that are not likely to be retained. True or false tests have long been criticized as being too superficial and too easy. Definitions as test items give children an opportunity to write or talk about what is true and what they know about it. Our lesson *Telling Tools* offers children eleven different ways to discuss anything.

Word Enhancement Effect

This phenomenon was first noted by Graf and Schacter (1985). They showed research subjects two words and asked them to make a sentence bringing the words together in some way. Later the subjects were asked to recall the words. They performed significantly better at this task than did a control group who were asked only to recall the words without making up a sentence using them.

Our *Language Wise* lesson *Word Sandwiches* gives children an opportunity to practice this strategy. This is a turn-taking game. The players take turns reading two words and then must quickly make up a sentence including these words. About twenty sets of words are offered. After these are used up we encourage you to take turns thinking of words for the other players to make into a sentence. Try this right now with these words.

Saturday grief _____

_____

_____

_____

notion eclipse _____

_____

_____

_____

endless glitter _____

_____

_____

_____

Our *Comparison and Contrast* lesson is a way of engaging the word enhancement effect. By considering two concepts in relation to one another, the child more richly encodes information about each, weaving them together, lending structure to each. The following is an example of a comparison and contrast of an *egg* and *clothing*. This example was obtained from a fifteen year old *Language Wise* client at the Read America clinic. Sandy was obsessed with fashion to the extent that it was difficult to get her to think or talk about anything else. Her therapist invited her to compare and contrast clothing with an egg. This is what she came up with.

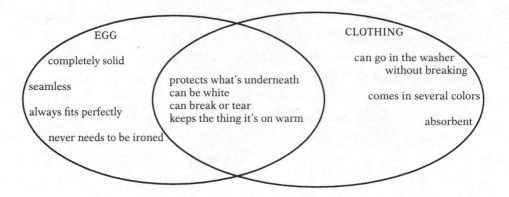

Sandy went on to write a very entertaining essay which was subsequently published in her high school newspaper. It's too long to reprint here, but the title, *Seamless Fashion*, gives you an idea of the content. The teacher who edits Sandy's school paper liked the piece so much that she invited Sandy to report for the paper the following year—this from a girl who was brought in for *Language Wise* therapy because she was flunking English class. You might remember that in chapter one our survey of parents and teachers using *Language Wise* activities revealed a ninety-four percent improvement in writing and a ninety-eight percent improvement in attitude about language arts activities. Sandy's article is a wonderful example of both.

Repetition and Spacing Effect

It has long been accepted that repetition of new material will improve learning. Russo and Parkin (1993) found that the benefits of repetition in presentation of material are increased if other material is presented in between the repeated material. Although the authors offer no explanation for this phenomenon, it is valuable information to teachers and parents regarding pacing lessons.

Context Effects

You're in the grocery store and the cashier looks very familiar. You say hello and inquire as to her well-being in that non-committal way that humans do that is meant to mean either, "I recognize you, how are you doing?" or "We don't know each other, but I'm very friendly. How are you?" She rings up your groceries, you pay and you leave. On the way home it hits you. Of course, she's your boss's daughter, whom you met at the company picnic. Seeing her in the context of the grocery store actually blocked your ability to realize where you knew her from. This is called a *context effect*.

In research conducted in 1970 (Light and Carter-Sobell) researchers found dramatic differences in results on tests based on whether the test item was embedded in the same or a different context than that in which it was taught.

As parents and teachers we need to assure that our children are able to cross contextual boundaries with the information we give them. The ability to do this is largely dependent on experience at doing it. If we don't expect and ask children to connect information up to contexts outside of those in which it was taught, we shouldn't be surprised when they can't do this. Our *Language Wise* games *Analogies* and *Connections* are recommended for this purpose.

Types of Information

The word *information* means exactly what it implies, to form within. Information comes in various sizes, shapes, and colors. For instance there is a difference between knowing *that* and knowing *how* (Ryle, 1949). I know that planes fly, but I know Chopin's *Impromptu*. I know when it was written. I would know it if I heard it played. I can hum it in my head. But, I do not know *how* to play it. I however know *how* to drive a car, but I don't know the principles *that* make it run. Typically what we know *that* is known explicitly. We can access it and talk about it easily enough. And what we know *how* is typically implicit. It is more difficult to access the various steps and to describe the processes involved. Riding a bike is a good example of this. Take a few minutes and write here a brief "how-to" on bike riding for my friend Nitchka from the planet Zingronia where they have no bicycles.

_____

_____

_____

_____

_____

_____

_____

_____

_____

_____

_____

_____

_____

_____

_____

How about that peddling action? It's difficult to describe, isn't it? Did you find you had to almost act it out to get all the moves right? You probably caught yourself skipping steps too. Now walk up to any adept bike riding seven year old and ask him why he doesn't fall over when he rides his bike. Nine out of ten of them wouldn't be about to answer this *that* question even though they know *how* to ride the bike just fine.

Different kinds of information are best learned in different ways. Let's have a look at some typical kinds of information that we humans try to commit to memory and how these are best learned.

Phonic Information—Learning Lists or "Songs"

When children first learn to count or to recite the ABCs they're committing to memory a rote and arbitrary sequence of sounds. I remember learning the words to a little song that went, "Maresy dotes and dosy dotes and little amsy divy, a kiddledy divy too wouldn't you?" when I was about five years old. Later I saw the song in writing and learned that it was correctly sung, "Mares eat oats and does eat oats, and little lambs eat ivy, a kid will eat ivy too, wouldn't you?" I had learned a phonic representation of the song that was almost, but not perfectly accurate. My daughter Mandy first learned the ABCs as, "aby, seedy," etc. Have you any songs that you sing happily along to on the radio, fully aware that what you're saying is gibberish? Phonic information is very easy to learn because it's catchy, it has a kind of rhythm to it, or can be set to one. Needless to say, accuracy is important. If you're going to learn the alphabet, it might as well be *the* alphabet, as in the ABCs and not the *aby seedys*. This kind of information is easily learned through rote rehearsal. Sing along or recite enough and you will know the words to the song or poem, the names of the presidents. Much phonic information can be learned with very little attention to the lesson. How did you learn all those songs you know by heart and sing along to on the radio? You heard them a lot, over and over again. You started to sing along to the parts you know. You learned more, and now, at the age of thirty-four you're stuck with the words to Don McLean's *American Pie*—whether you like it or not.

Episodic Information

Episodic information is an individual's autobiographical account of his experiences. It is a running, sequential record of everything that ever happened to you. We tend to recall more literally that which is novel. I remember for instance that for many years during my childhood my family travelled to Sanibel Island for two weeks each October to celebrate my father's birthday. I have very few specific memories of these vacations, but for one year in particular. On that particular trip I was photographed on the beach with my poodle Sasha for the cover of a magazine about shells. About other years I remember only that we golfed and swam and ate out every night. I remember that particular event because it stood out among the other events of the collective Sanibel Island birthday vacations.

Procedural Information

Much of what we do in life is procedural. Driving a car, eating in a restaurant, making a phone call, writing a check and riding a bike are all examples of procedural tasks that most of us engage in on a regular basis. At some point in time we may have had some explicit instruction in the skills involved in the task, but with expertise has come automaticity. Again, if you're asked to write down the steps involved in riding a bicycle you have to think consciously about the task, while actually doing the task requires little or no conscious thought. The same is often true of learning procedural tasks. We tend to learn them very well with little or no conscious attention, simply by repeated observation. We call this *latent learning*.

It's important to emphasize that procedural information is not just motor skills. Let's do a non-motor procedural task. Organize the following words according to weight from the lightest to the heaviest.

cat, cigarette, boulder, automobile, leaf, marble, empty coffee cup, spoon

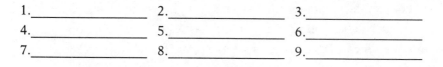

1._____   2._____   3._____
4._____   5._____   6._____
7._____   8._____   9._____

Now explain the procedure you used to do this.

_____

_____

_____

_____

_____

_____

Prospective Information

Your aging Aunt Iris calls to ask you to pick her up and take her for her annual dental cleaning. The phone call goes on and on with much pride in the fact that she still has all of her own teeth. Of course you'll take her and yes you'll stop by the yarn store on the way home. Arrangements are made for Thursday at 10:00. Bless her heart you think as you thankfully deposit the receiver back on its hook. Fleetingly you think of adding this to the calendar hanging by the phone, but it's Monday, and Thursday is just three days from now. Instead you return to preparation of the evening meal, cordon bleu. Life goes on. It's a typical week, Thursday comes and goes, it's Friday morning. The phone rings. It's Aunt Iris calling to say that since you must have been too busy to take her to the dentist yesterday, she's made another appointment for next Tuesday. "Is that convenient?" Your heart sinks. You're a loser, a rat, a rotten miserable niece. Yes, of course you'll take her. You write it on the calendar—in fuchsia marker. Within a few minutes you're feeling better. You'll take her out to lunch too. You call Billy's and order a pizza with extra mushrooms and carry on reviewing the Robinson case, which you've brought home from work. Your fourteen year old son Harry arrives home from football practice. You wonder if he'll remember that it's trash night or if you'll have to remind him. The pizza arrives. You eat as Harry updates you on the events at school, how unfair Mr. Haroldson was about his term project grade. You're still wondering if Harry will remember the trash or if you'll have to remind him. The conversation turns to Harry needing a ride to the mall music store where he plans a purchase of the new *Barenaked Ladies* CD. You shudder at the name and inquire how he plans to pay for this purchase. "With my chore money of course," he responds. "Oh, it's trash night, got to go take out the trash," he says as he pops a kiss on your cheek and dashes for the back door.

   Your task to recall Aunt Iris's dental date and Harry's task to recall the trash each Tuesday night are examples of *prospective memory*. Prospective memory is very different from other sorts of memory as it deals with recalling an event that has not yet happened. It is memory of an action yet to be taken. The two events have some differences. Aunt Iris's dentist appointment was a one-time visit, while the trash event reoccurs weekly. Another difference is in the way the two are perceived by the appointed task doers. Taking Aunt Iris to the dentist is a favor, while the trash has been made a job in the imaginary household depicted above—a job with a monetary reward attached to it. Just as the mom in our story remembered to bring home the Robinson case, *her job*, Harry remembered to take out the trash, but he might not have done had the CD purchase and the need for money for such not come into the conversation.

While we don't advocate monetary or other rewards in most situations, proscriptive memory for tasks that have been designated as jobs may be an appropriate introduction to monetary rewards. This scenario mimics life, at least life in this era, in a capitalistic society. In addition, there is some research evidence that in the case of designated jobs, monetary reward can improve prospective memory and in turn verbal intelligence. In 1977 Meacham and Singer conducted a study of this which was repeated with the same results in 1982. They asked college students to send a postcard to a particular address on a particular day for eight weeks. Half the participants were asked to send the postcards on particular dates and were offered no feedback. The other half were paid for each postcard that arrived on time. The unpaid group missed an average of 2.1 of the eight cards, while the paid group missed an average of 1.4 cards. We urge caution here and offer some recommendations.

1. The job should offer assistance to others, not just the job doer. Getting good grades for instance is not a job. It will help only one person in the end—the person with the A.

2. Don't overdo the job thing. Everyone living in the house should be expected to participate to some extent. Expect some *favors* in addition to the *jobs*. Use language to denote this: "Don't forget it's your trash night," as opposed to, "I'll be home late tonight, so would you do me a favor when you get home and fold the laundry on the couch and put it away?"

3. It's one thing to remind someone about their job every now and then, but on the whole if it's their job they should be responsible for remembering it. As I used to tell my kids when they were younger and less responsible, "It isn't helpful if I have to nag or remind you." Make your children take responsibility. Don't pay them if they don't do the job. That's what happens at work.

4. Don't use this technique on children under about eleven or twelve years of age. There is considerable research evidence that rewards do not improve and may actually be detrimental to performance at a young age (Cuvo, 1974; Deci, 1975).

Semantic Information aka Knowledge

Semantic knowledge is our mental model of the world (Tulving, 1985). It makes it possible for us to devise cognitive representations of the things, situations, facts and events of the world, as we recall them from the past, experience them in the present, and imagine them in the future. Through these models, these cognitive structures, we can stop having to relearn or rediscover information. It is structuralized for safe keeping. These mental structures are also the stuff upon which we hang new information coming into our realm of experience.

Clearly the various types of information one commits to memory are related in some ways. It's not our intention to segregate these kinds of information in the minds of parents and teachers. We intend only that those who teach children have an understanding of the subtle and not so subtle differences in what they ask of the children they teach and how these ultimately interrelate.

Implicit and Explicit Memory and Top Down and Bottom Up Instruction

There is considerable evidence that there are two kinds of memories for semantic information, *implicit* and *explicit*. Explicit memories are those that are specific. Educators call explicit lessons *bottom up* instruction. All the parts are used to construct the big picture. Implicit memories are conceptual. Educators call these lessons top down instruction. The big picture is presented and the parts are assumed or discovered by the learner. Various theories about the best approach abound in the field of education.

Learning Styles

Many educators believe that the decision about whether to apply the top down or bottom up approach depends upon the learner. They believe that some learners are top down learners while some are bottom up learners. While there is some research evidence that this is true, there are two fundamental problems with this.

There is no evidence that individuals are inherently top down or bottom up learners. How do we know we're not creating a bias toward a particular approach to problem solving based upon the experiences we set before our students?

Regardless of the kind of learner we have before us, there will be particular material that we must present to him that is best learned from one direction or the other. What then? Do we simply follow the child over the cliffs of failure, or do we teach him as the material dictates?

Theoretical Orientation

Some educators believe that one or the other of these approaches should be used exclusively. The kind of approach used tends to swing back and forth depending upon what's in vogue at the moment. The back to basics people are bottom uppers, while the holistic education people tend to be top downers. Some educators see the value in attacking instruction from both ends. Maria Montessori, Italian physician and developer of the Montessori method of education, wrote of *cosmic education*—her notion that children should be presented with the whole picture and then instructed in the various skills and information that make up that picture. This approach is prudent as, with the conceptual aspects of the material made transparent to the child, he is able to see where the instruction in skills and information is going—the need for it, how it fits together, etc. The big picture adds stability to lessons by giving them a structure upon which to hang. While top down instruction is like solving a puzzle with the box lid and no pieces, and bottom up instruction is like having the puzzle pieces and no lid, *cosmic education* gives the student the box lid and the puzzle pieces. While this approach takes into account the nature of the learner, the child, in its application, it fails to take into account one other critically important component—the nature of the material. The kind of information one is passing on plays a critical role in everything that follows. To be able to teach a child about something, one must understand its nature—its *essence*.

Essential Education

Much is known about the nature of the child as a learner. Research has uncovered many secrets withheld from us for centuries. The next millennium promises to be a brighter place for the child as he sets about his business of growing and learning. But we must remember that learning is an interaction between the learner and the material to be learned. Understanding the nature of that material to be taught is just as critical to our success as understanding the nature of the learner. Just as the learner has a nature which we've uncovered through psychoeducational inquiry, so too does the material we wish to teach him. Every thing we could ever want to teach a child has a nature. If our instruction is to be *memorable* we must consider carefully what it is that we ask of children before we set out our lessons and pose our orienting questions—we must understand the problem as well as the problem solver. In the next chapter we'll examine problem solving through logical reasoning and creative processes.

CHAPTER SIX

PROBLEM SOLVING

LOGICAL REASONING AND CREATIVITY

In this chapter you will learn

The three elements of every problem.

How to teach your child to attend to the relevant information in order to solve a problem.

How to represent problems.

If your child is an *approacher* or *avoider* of problems.

How to avoid raising a child with *functional fixedness*.

The part of *inference* and *inductive reasoning* in problem solving.

How to form and use *power questions.*

What *creativity* is.

How to raise a *problem finder*.

From our very earliest weeks of life we encounter them. As we breathe our last breath they still plague us. They come in many forms. While most are merely an inconvenience, some can be life threatening. Many come and go without our conscious attention. Some are even fun. Cats and dogs and elephants have them too, though not nearly as complex a variety. Some of the ones humans have we cause ourselves. These can be the hardest to solve. We all learn from them, though some of us learn more and faster than others.

Problem Solving

One of the things that sets us humans apart from the rest of the animal kingdom is our keen ability to solve problems. We are indeed masters of the game. A problem is when you want to reach a certain goal but the path is not obvious (Squire, 1992). How we illuminate the path between where we are and where we want to be depends on many factors. Our ability to do this so much better than the cats and dogs and elephants is largely a result of our ability to symbolize life, to speak, to imagine, to visualize our world in as many ways as the mind will churn out, trying these on like hats. The information we have to choose from in so doing is gained from all of history as we know it, and as we can learn it from written record. It is gained from imaginary quests into the future, bringing back as many possibilities as we can carry. All the world is our stage when a problem confronts us, and we are both director and star.

Though each problem that life hands us is unique in many ways, each is the same in some ways. Every problem has three elements (Davidson et al. 1994): the *initial state*, which is where you are; the *goal state*, which is where you want to be; and the *obstacles*, which is what prevents you from being there. If, for instance, you're the single parent of three children trying to buy a home on one income, your initial state is tenant, your goal state is homeowner, and your obstacle is not enough money. If on the other hand you're a single parent who's an architect earning $280,000 a year, and still can't afford a home, your obstacle may be self-control with your finances. And in another scenario—if you're a single parent architect who can't decide where she wants to live— you don't have a problem at all, just a decision to be made. But we'll talk more about decisions later in the chapter.

Why are some people better at solving problems than others? In the next several sections we'll explore the variables involved in problem solving and how these may affect one's success at solving problems.

Attending to the Relevant Information

It would be lovely if problems were presented to us in neat little boxes, isolated from the rest of our world so that we could attend only to them, solving them diligently and then carrying on with the rest of our lives. You can't get the peanut butter jar open for instance, and all else freezes until you've managed to solve the problem. Ha! More likely there's a four year old crying, "But I'm hungry!" And of course the doorbell *and* the phone ring. Meanwhile the bath you're running overflows while you're dealing with the phone call and the still tightly sealed peanut butter jar. You're only hope is that the person at the door is a big guy with strong forearms and a broader grip than yours. Sometimes it's difficult just to recognize the relevant information. You run a dry cleaning business and suddenly you notice that business is off by 27% from this time last year. The first question is—*why?* Is it the staff, the market, the location? What's changed? If we don't isolate these factors and determine which is actually the problem, we spend all our energy on the symptoms of the problem rather than the problem itself. It may be that you need a change of staff. Or some staff development for your existing staff. These are different problems altogether and would be dealt with in different ways. Children make these same mistakes in the classroom every day. They get caught up in the fact that they have work to do and the work not yet done is viewed as the problem, when in reality the problem is on the page—20 multiplication problems. And of course if the child is unable to do these problems the problem is altogether different. Now the problem is getting some instruction in the skills needed to be able to solve the problems on the page.

Children need careful training in isolating the actual problem. How the adults in their lives treat their own problems, and how they redirect children when they become confused about what their problems are, will determine how good children are at isolating their own problems as they arise. I saw a very clear example of this in a classroom a few months ago. A child of about eleven wanted a particular color paint for an art project he was working on. He went to the art storage closet and spotted it on the top shelf, some two feet from his reach. He went to fetch the teacher and said, "I need the purple paint." She looked him in the eye and said, "What's the problem?" He repeated his original statement. "I need the purple paint." And she said, "That's not a problem. Now, what *is* the problem?" He said, "I can't reach it." "Oh," she said, "Do you have a plan?" "Um, well yes," he answered. "I could get your chair." "Good plan," she said, "thank you for asking. Please be careful." As I sat taking notes I thought how fortunate these children were to have this teacher. Later in the day I did a demonstration reading lesson for some of the kindergarten teachers at this school. I was to work with five five year old children whom I had never seen before, in their classroom while their teacher and three other kindergarten teachers watched. The children were on the playground with the classroom assistants while the teachers were setting up a table and chairs for me to work at with the children. They were telling me all the problems they'd been having trying to work with a group of five children every day for twenty minutes. "The other children disturb us during the lesson," they explained. "It's a big problem." "What do they do?" I asked. "Oh they need this or that. Someone needs a shoe tied. A pencil needs sharpening." After the demonstration I talked with them at length about their interruptions. They thought they had one problem—children interrupting the lesson. What they actually had were four distinct problems. Once they realized this they were able to solve each easily in the following ways.

1. Lots of sharpened pencils were put out each day to solve the problem of the teacher being interrupted to sharpen a pencil.

2. A bit of red nail polish was applied to the stop button on the classroom tape recorders and a bit of green on the start button, to solve the problem of the teacher having to start and stop the tape recorder.

3. Jason was appointed as classroom shoelace tier, an honor he seemed happy to accept, to solve the problem of the teacher being interrupted to tie shoes. I also predicted that the other children would learn faster from Jason, a slow moving beginner at shoe tying, than from a teacher who was rushed.

4. Everyone was given a strip of red *Avery dots*. When there was an altercation of any sort between two children the child who was upset (usually both children) was to put a red dot on his desk. This was a reminder to tell the teacher what happened later on when she reconvened the whole class. Predicting that everyone would have a problem so that they could place a red dot on their desk, we also gave each child a green dot which indicated no problems.

Checking back a week later all four teachers reported the lessons were going well.

Good problem solving like this requires self-monitoring. We call this kind of self-monitoring metacognition—*thinking about thinking*. The ability to do this is largely dependent upon how expert you are at the skills surrounding the problem you're attempting to solve. Glaser and Chi (1988) found that the more expert one is at a particular skill, the better able one is to perform metacognitive self-monitoring while performing those skills. It would follow that if we want our children to be able to self-monitor during problem solving, we must help them to perform very well at what we ask of them. Additionally we should be modeling metacognitive processes in our instruction.

Representing the Problem

Once we've isolated what the actual problem is, we begin to form mental representations of the problem. How well we do this will affect how successful we are at eventually solving the problem (Donely & Ashcraft, 1992; Mayer, 1982, 1985). Problem solvers use lists, matrices, hierarchical trees, graphs and visual images to represent problems. Different representations work better than others. If for instance you're planning a party and need to get an idea of how many people you should buy food and drink for, a list is the best plan. If however you need to transport these same people to a football game after the party and you have five cars available for the ride, a matrix would be helpful.

Approaches to the Problem

Once the problem solver has isolated and represented the problem it's time to approach the problem. The two most common courses of approach are heuristics and analogies. In a heuristic approach, the problem solver attempts to break the problem down into constituent parts and then sets about solving each of these. In an analogy approach, the problem solver seeks an analogous problem and considers how this was solved, or how it might be solved and then how that relates back to the problem at hand. Researchers (Keane 1988; Lawson & Lawson, 1993) have noted that the use of analogies in problem solving can lead to creative breakthroughs. We'll have a close look at creative problem solving later in this chapter. Other researchers (Halpern et al. 1990) have found that the success of using analogies in problem solving is heavily dependent upon the ability to isolate a pure and accurate analogy to the problem. Holyoak and Koh (1987) and Reed (1993) have found in clinical studies of the use of analogies in problem solving that people often fail to see the analogy between a past resolved problem and a new problem. They fail to recognize the structural differences in forming these analogies. Our lesson *Analogies* helps children to discover and understand how to form and use analogies.

Other Problems We Have Solving Problems

In addition to difficulties people have in forming heuristics and analogies, numerous challenges get in the way of us humans solving problems. In this section we'll explore some of these.

Approachers and Avoiders

Some problem solving goes awry when the problem solver fails to approach the problem at all. According to motivation theorist David McClelland (1987), the strongest reason for this is that the problem contains too much novelty—there is not enough about the problem that fits into the individual's existing schema. If this happens frequently in the developing years, the individual may in time become an a*voider* rather than an *approacher* of problems.

Another force driving the development of an avoidance reaction is fear. Individuals fearing failure in problem solving scenarios may resolve this fear by actively avoiding the problem (Mehribian, 1970; Sorrentino & Sheppard, 1978). Such fears develop as a result of repeated threats, implied or real, in problem solving situations. Such threats can come from parents, teachers or peers. Fear of success is equally compelling, the implication being, "If I succeed, much will be expected of me."

Yet another reason driving the development of an avoidance reaction may be learned tolerance for the anxiety associated with unresolved problems. As we discussed in chapter two, it's the natural state of man to attempt to make his environment as pleasant as possible—to form a best fit between himself and the rest of the world. Sometimes people learn to accept an imperfect or uncomfortable fit instead. They come to the conclusion that it's more trouble than it's worth to them to attempt to improve their lot by solving a few problems. I recently read a quote in Ann Landers' column that exemplifies this perfectly. The letter had been written by a real estate agent who was complaining that you just can't help some people. He had asked his client what area of town he was interested in. The answer displayed a distinct approach to solving the problem of finding a new house. "Well," he answered, "I don't want to live in the East, West, North or South." Clearly, there was no risk of him being disappointed by the remaining choices.

Decisions, Decisions, Decisions

Some people fail to solve problems successfully simply because they fail to make a decision at the end of the process. Oftentimes in life, there is not one, but numerous alternatives available to solving a problem. We weigh the alternatives, the pros and cons, and then decide on a course of action. In research conducted by Frisch and Clemen (1994) and by Smyth (1994), much of this determination is based on opinion alone. When people fail to make a decision in a problem solving situation, they lose by default, and the decision is made for them by others, or simply by circumstances taking over the situation.

Mental Set

Mental set is defined as mindless rigidity that blocks problem solving. Specifically it is the inability to bust out of the picture one has of the overall problem. I recently saw a three year old struggling with this very challenge—and winning. He was pouring marbles from a large plastic beaker into three small plastic bowls. The challenge was to fill the bowls without spilling the marbles. The teacher had intentionally designed the lesson so that the bowls were all very full when all the marbles were poured out. The three year old, Tommy, had become quite adept at pouring dry substances, but had not yet encountered the very full variable requiring this level of precision. With every attempt he spilled the last few marbles and got very angry at this. Finally, after numerous attempts, he filled the three bowls about three quarters full, leaving about twenty marbles remaining in the bottom of the plastic beaker. Then, looking around to make sure no one was watching, he reached in and placed the marbles one at a time in the bowls, stacking them ever so carefully. Our *Language Wise* lesson *Connections* teaches children how to break up *mental set* and *functional fixedness*, discussed next.

Functional Fixedness

Functional fixedness is when the functions or uses we assign to objects tend to remain rigidly fixed. The classic study of this phenomenon was conducted by Duncker in 1945 and is known as *Duncker's candle experiment*. Subjects were given a candle, a box of matches and a box of thumbtacks and asked to affix the candle to the wall and light it. No other materials were allowed. Participants in the study tried all the things you're probably thinking of right now. They tried melting wax and sticking the candle to the wall. They tried using the thumbtacks to hang it on the wall. The resolution comes in removing the fixed functions we think of for the available material, and *voila*—we have a matchbox thumbtacked to the wall as a tiny shelf upon which to rest a candle.

Child development researchers tell us that children are far less functionally fixed than adults. I recently watched a four year old who wanted to put all the sand in his sandbox into his wagon but hadn't a shovel with which to move it. He started to use his hands as a shovel and was making steady progress. As he was moving about at his task he lost a shoe. He stared at it for a moment and then picked it up and began scooping sand into it and dumping it into the wagon. Something we do to children as they pass through childhood must discourage this kind of free thinking. Perhaps it is social protocol that scares us out of such spontaneous and effective use of our environment. In addition to our *Connections* lesson mentioned earlier, our *Brainstorming* lesson can be quite effective at reducing functional fixedness. In one of the items, the child is asked to think of all the uses he can for a piece of yellow ribbon. Try this yourself right now. Write down as many ideas as you can generate. You'll enjoy it. It's like therapy after a long day of following policy and procedure at work.

_____

_____

_____

_____

_____

_____

_____

_____

_____

_____

_____

_____

_____

_____

_____

_____

_____

_____

_____

_____

_____

_____

_____

_____

_____

_____

_____

_____

_____

_____

_____

That's probably enough. If you want to keep going move to a piece of paper.

Logical Reasoning

Logical reasoning is to infer logical consequences from available information (Evans, 1993). The way in which this is done changes dramatically throughout the life span. It's important to understand what can be reasonably expected of a child from whom one expects logical reasoning. The person best known for sorting out the developmental stages of logical reasoning is Swiss biologist and psychologist Jean Piaget. John Flavell, who has been referenced throughout this book, is a follower of Piaget's theories, and has done much of the work supporting and adjusting Piaget's original work. As we progress through this section we'll refer to research conducted by Flavell and others examining the theories developed by Piaget. According to Piaget's *theory of cognitive development*, children follow a fairly consistent developmental track in the area of cognitive development and logical reasoning. Piaget isolated four stages of cognitive development.

Sensorimotor Stage (Birth to Two)

At birth the infant's ability to problem solve is largely dependent upon how well his reflexes are operating. The ability to nurse, orient the eyes, and cry out in pain are all managed by reflex. In the first few months of life, the child begins to replace reflexes with intentional actions upon and reactions to his environment. His activities are no longer random. He becomes a player in the world of cause and effect. Baldwin (1968) described the abilities of this period of development as:

1. Understanding that the information received from different senses relates to the same object. The baby learns that the music he *hears* is coming from the teddy bears he *sees* circling overhead.

2. Recognizing that the world is a permanent place, independent of the child perceiving it.

3. Executing goal directed behavior. The young baby notices that his flailing hand hits upon the circling teddy bears, and so he learns to direct his hand *to* the teddy bears.

Preoperational Thought (Two to Six)

With *preoperational thought* children begin to be able to symbolize. They learn that things can *stand for* other things. The ability to symbolize offers the developing child many new opportunities.

1. As we illustrated in chapter one, language is a symbolic representation of the things in our world. It is in the preoperational stage of development that the child begins to learn and use language.

2. The ability to symbolize allows the child to cast his mind back to the past remembered.

3. Symbolizing allows children to think of places and people not present, but remembered.

John Flavell's research identified cognitive limitations of the *preoperational thought* stage of development, which prevent children from being fully logical at this age, and should be understood and considered by their parents and teachers. According to Flavell children's ability to symbolize in this stage is limited to the physical world. They are not yet capable of extending this to concepts. Flavell also found that children remain *egocentric* throughout this stage of cognitive development. Flavell defined this as *the awareness of self without an awareness of the needs and interests of others.* The preoperational child is the center of his own universe. This is especially noticeable in his language, which consists of largely monologue or dual monologue when more than one child is involved. The following is a real dual monologue recorded at a school in Orlando last week.

> Four year old Susie: "I have a dollie."
> Five year old George: "My finger hurts."
> Susie: "My dollie is Tammy."
> George: "Vroom."
> Susie: "I went to see Mickey Mouse."

Flavell also found that children at this stage tend to *centrate.* They focus on one aspect of a situation or object. This centration causes children to be very bad problem solvers in certain situations. The classic experiment in this involved making determinations about whether the water in a tall, slim glass would fit into a short, fat glass. Children at this stage focus on the height of the glass, failing to consider the width.

Concrete Operations (Six to Eleven)

Sometime around their sixth birthday children begin to develop *operational thought*. Where the last stage of cognitive development limited them to activities upon the physical world, they now become able to carry out *mental* activities as well. This capability allows them to use concepts such as fairness—to others as well as themselves—and to manage more than one attribute at a time, understanding that a short, fat container will hold about the same amount of water as a tall, slim container. They can understand concepts like multiplication, seeing that the principle is merely addition in multiples, and they can begin to imagine the future as well as remember the past.

Formal Operations (Twelve to Adulthood)

Where concrete operations dealt with objects in the environment and concepts, *formal operations* deals with more abstract thoughts such as alternatives, possibilities, propositions and hypotheses. An important aspect of this stage is that it is not a given. Not all adolescents reach this level of cognitive development. In a study conducted by McClosky, Caramazza and Green (1980), researchers found that children who had had formal courses in science and math did better at tests of formal operations than children who had not had such courses.

These problems are elusive not only for some older children; considerable research has shown that children as young as six can succeed at problems of formal operations with proper instruction (Case, 1974). Children in this study received only four days of instruction in how to isolate variables and test and keep track of possibilities.

Deductive Reasoning

As we said at the beginning of this section *logical reasoning* is to infer logical consequences from available information (Evans, 1993). This can be done de*ductively* or *inductively*. When we reason deductively we make inferences from the general to the particular. This is top down processing. So knowing for instance that men are paid more than women on the average, when we hear of a doctor, we tend to think of a man.

This perfectly exemplifies one of the problems that people have in doing deductive reasoning. Deductive reasoning fails when we have a *belief bias. Men make more money than women. Doctors make a lot of money. Sam is a doctor, therefore, Sam is a man.*

People also struggle with deductive reasoning when the problem is stated in a negative. *Today is not Tuesday so you cannot go bowling. If I cannot go bowling today is not Tuesday.* Think how this illogical conclusion might have been avoided by stating the problem positively. *On Tuesday you can go bowling.*

Wason and Johnson-Laird (1972) found that people have more difficulty when problems requiring deductive reasoning are *abstractly stated. (Example) If an object is red, then it is rectangular. This object is not rectangular, therefore, it is not red.* These researchers more than doubled the subjects' failure rate by stating simple problems abstractly.

Constructing one model of the premise can interfere with deductive reasoning. You are invited to meet Bob at the theater at 8:00. You go to the theater and no Bob. You wait—it's 8:10, 8:20, 8:30 and still no Bob. You go home. Bob is a scoundrel? No, you had only one model of a theater in your world view. In fact Bob was at the performing arts theater enjoying *Riverdance* in a $125 seat, wondering what happened to you.

Many people demonstrate a distinct *failure to transfer old knowledge to the problem* when applying deductive reasoning. In a 1991 study (Samon) researchers found that even students of logic in a philosophy class failed to use their skills at logic in solving similar problems in another context.

Inductive Reasoning

Inductive reasoning is to infer from the particular to the general. It is bottom up processing. A five year old is playing on the playground with his classmates. A golden haired girl comes up and pushes him from his swing. He regains his footing, puts his hands on his hips, looks her square in the eyes and says, "Dummy!" She retreats to the seesaws. Later that day he is working at the art center in his classroom. All the paintbrushes are currently in use by other children. He looks round the room and spots a feather brought in for *share time* by a classmate. He fetches it and is just about to immerse it in yellow tempera when his teacher snatches it from his poised hand. "Dummy!" he says. A half hour later as he sits waiting to see the school head for a long talk on manners and respect, he has learned that induction is a hazardous activity requiring more than one trial.

This youngster *overgeneralized* the effect of the word *dummy* by quite a bit. Another failure we encounter in inductive reasoning is in *undergeneralization*. At the Read America clinic we see lots of students who suffer from chronic under-generalization. They read the word *green* in one sentence and then in the next cannot tell you what sound is in the middle of *feet*. Oftentimes these children suffer from a lack of awareness that the world is somewhat predictable—that there are patterns that can be used over and over again.

Power Questions

Our *Language Wise* lessons will help children prevent and overcome some of the causes of failure at deductive and inductive reasoning. In addition to these we suggest some rather rigorous questioning procedures that we call *power questions*. You probably recall that in the last chapter we recommended orienting tasks to get the child's attention. Power questions are a way of maintaining control over the orientation, and manipulating your child's perception of the area being investigated. As a point of departure here we want to point out that in recent years there has been some focus on the use of *open ended questions* in education. An open ended question is a question that allows the answerer to go in any one of many directions with his answer. While there is a time and place for open ended questions, they are greatly oversold in educational circles as being the best way to inspire thoughtful or creative answers. While an open ended question does indeed allow for thoughtful and creative answers, it also allows the child to determine the level of complexity of the answer. It puts the question *in his court*. This is fine some of the time, but there are many occasions when we want and need more control in questioning children. In contrast, a *closed question* requires a specific answer and allows the questioner to control the level of complexity of the answer based upon the formation of the question. Following is an example of open and closed questions.

Open ended question: What did you do at school today?
Answer: I played on the playground.

Closed question: What work did you do at school today?
Answer: I worked on multiplication and we wrote a story.

Another guideline in forming questions is to always require that the child answer the question you asked. Children are very good at avoiding the issues and changing the topic entirely. It's important that parents and teachers keep to the topic. We call this ruthless questioning. A few weeks back my daughter promised to baby-sit for our neighbors. Their house was being treated for termites so she agreed to watch over Trevor and Laura here at our house. They were playing in our pool and Mandy was lying in the sun nearby and reading her history book. I looked out to check on things just as events took a downward slide. Laura (six) slapped Trevor (four) right across the face with an inflatable dragon just moments before Mandy looked up. From my vantage point I saw the whole thing and it was indeed a planned encounter. Mandy's question, "Laura, why is Trevor crying?" Laura's answer, "I was on the steps." Mandy (only fifteen and not as gifted at ruthless questioning as her mom) now assumed that Trevor was wailing over some self-inflicted injury. "Come on out Trevor. Come over here and sit by me for a while." Needless to say I intervened with an eyewitness testimony and some expert problem solving techniques. There's no way I was going to let Trevor get punished for his sister's mistreatment of him. On my arrival poolside I pointed out to Laura that she had not answered Mandy's question. Again she repeated, "I was on the steps." So I said, "Mandy's question was why is Trevor crying?" "Oh," said Laura, "Um, the dragon hit him in the face." It wasn't until she'd finished the statement that Laura, still clutching the dragon, knew she was done for. She accompanied Trevor to the deck chair where she waited until he was calm and could return to the pool.

There are several different specific kinds of questioning that can be employed *ruthlessly*. Following is a list of these, the purpose for each, and an example of each.

POWER QUESTIONING

Be Ruthless—Always make sure that you get an answer to *the* question you asked.

Progressive Questioning—The child's answer reveals what aspect of the original question he didn't understand. Form another question based on this and continue. *(Example) You ask a twelve year old, "What were the causes of the Civil War?" He answers, "General Lee and General Grant." He has revealed that he doesn't understand what you mean by 'cause'. Ask, "What was one problem that started the war?"*

Dissective Questioning—Breaking a large, general question into basic elemental parts with many questions unfolding. *(Example) It's the first week of school. You've gone over the playground rules four days in a row. You want to be sure that your class of eight year olds understands the rules. Instead of asking, "What are the rules for the playground?" you ask, "Who can tell me the rule about the swings?" From there you progress to another rule, and another.*

Specific Questioning—Targeting one particular question inside a larger, more general issue. This is intended to focus the discussion. *(Example) You walk outside where your three sons have been playing with four neighborhood boys. Your youngest son is bleeding heavily from the nose. Instead of asking, "What happened?" you ask, "Who was nearest to Tommy when he was hurt?" Chances are whoever was nearest inflicted the injury, but if not, at least he had the best vantage point.*

Marginal Questioning—Asking a question on the fringe of the issue. This is intended to broaden the discussion. *(Example) Your ten year old is going on incessantly about his new video game. You want to let him express himself, but it's been twenty-five minutes and it's time to broaden the discussion. You're thinking that computers would be a better topic. "Do they have your game on CD-ROM yet?"*

Reductive Absurd Questioning—Progress from a child's statement that doesn't seem absurd to him and reduce it in increments to an absurd question. *(Example) You're picking your seven year old up at the end of the school day. As you drive up to the pickup spot you notice a distinct downward turn to his mouth. He gets in the car and announces, "I hate my teacher." Instead of saying, "Oh, you do not. You like your teacher. She's very nice," and completely invalidating his problem you say, "Well you must be really mad at her." "Yup," he says crossing his arms on his chest. "What did she do?" This allows him to state his case. Often hearing it from his own lips will help him realize it wasn't the crime he thought it was at the time. After he's done you continue, "So, you'd probably be pretty happy if she moved away and wasn't your teacher any more?" "Yup," he confirms. "Or if she was ill and you had a substitute for a long time?" "Yup." "Or if she died and you got a new teacher?" Most children will realize the absurdity of "I hate my teacher" at this point.*

Obvious Questioning—Target a specific aspect or situation relative to a more general statement, which makes it obvious that the general statement doesn't hold up. *(Example) Your thirteen year old is at a stage in her development where she thinks it's her personal responsibility to tell people how to live. Her friend Sarah has told her what you term a 'white lie', but she's decided it's grounds for termination of the friendship. You have a fleeting thought that maybe you should stay out of it, but that last statement, "YOU SHOULD NEVER LIE!" is really bothering you. You say, "So if a murderer broke into our house and I hid, and he asked where I was, you would tell him the truth?"*

Creativity

To create, to really *create*, we would have to have the power to make something from nothing. The alchemists of the Dark and Middle Ages tampered with such concepts. In the modern world we understand that although we can turn energy and matter into other forms, we cannot truly create. The accepted definition of creativity is to reorganize existing elements or ideas in a novel way (David Perkins, 1994, 1996). A new house was recently built on our street. We met our new neighbors on one of their construction inspections. As the house neared completion the painters set about their task. The color that emerged was a deep teal green—not just the trim, but the walls as well. Many neighbors were un-happy with the outcome. As the color went on we all assumed it was a primer paint, soon to be covered with some nice color like *marble white*, *sea shell*, *dove grey*, or *bisque*. The green remained uncovered for two weeks, and then to our shock, they moved in—with their primer still unpainted? No, teal it was to be. At the McGuinness house we struggled with the reality that we hated the color. Not only because we're fair and reasonable people, but also because it was the exact same color as our carpet! Somehow it was just wrong on a house. When other neighbors began to inquire of them on their choice of color, the lady of the house explained that her husband is very *creative*.

Most researchers in the field of cognition agree that to be considered cre-ative, the newly organized elements of ideas must be valued by a significant num-ber of people (Margaret Boden, 1996). So it is not enough to paint your house a color that no one has ever painted a house before. The result must be appreci-ated. Real creativity, the valued kind, is a highly sought-after commodity in today's world. Teachers, universities and employers alike place great value on recruitment of creative minds. There isn't a field of endeavor that doesn't value creative insight.

Analogies

What processes underlie the creative reorganization of variables into a new and valued way of looking or doing? According to some researchers (Koestler, 1964; Hesse, 1988) most creative moments involve the recognition of a novel analogy between two previously unrelated concepts. William Harvey's observation that the heart is like a pump, for instance, was entirely different from previous con-cepts of the heart, and inspired a metamorphosis in physiology. Not only did this analogy drive the vascular research that followed, but it also spurred other such physiological connections such as seeing the liver as a filter and the brain as a control center. How is it that some people are able to make such analogies and others are not? Consider the variables. Think of the heart and what springs to mind—blood, tissue? These thoughts are limited to physical attributes. Moving on you may think, warm, sticky—more physical attributes. This kind of *mental set* (mentioned earlier in the chapter) limits our perception of the heart. Now stop thinking in terms of attributes and move on to function. What have you got? Blood being *pumped* through the body. A big part of the trick to analogies is to be able to think in terms of any quality of that to which we wish to form an analogy. When one takes an analogies test, or does our *Language Wise* lesson *Analogies*, one is led to some extent by the stimulus. For instance, *dog is to bark as cat is to*_____, begs a *meow*, as we are led and limited by the notion of the *sound* the thing makes. When analogies are drawn in life, rather than in a game, we have the world to draw from, all of its forms and functions. We're not guided or limited by the variables in an analogy; we can form our own analogy with the world as our playground.   What if the problem were dog is to bark as _____ is to _____? Take a few moments to come up with several answers.

Dog is to bark as _____ is to _____.
Dog is to bark as _____ is to _____.
Dog is to bark as _____ is to _____.
Dog is to bark as _____ is to _____.
Dog is to bark as _____ is to _____.
Dog is to bark as _____ is to _____.
Dog is to bark as _____ is to _____.
Dog is to bark as _____ is to _____.
Dog is to bark as _____ is to _____.
Dog is to bark as _____ is to _____.

You've probably exhausted the possibilities by this time. Have you come up with anything creative? Some of you have no doubt moved on to inanimate objects that make noise such as dog is to bark as train is to whistle. That's kind of fun! But what else have you done? If you haven't yet come up with something you think is especially creative, fear not. The chapter is young and so are we. In Harvey's observation that the heart is like a pump he threw off the confines of thinking in terms of physical attributes and noticed the functional attributes of the heart in seeking his analogies. Now take a moment to continue on with your search for analogies, asking yourself—what is a bark to a dog other than just a sound? What is the function of a bark for a dog?

Dog is to bark as _____ is to _____.

Dog is to bark as _____ is to _____.

Dog is to bark as _____ is to _____.

Dog is to bark as _____ is to _____.

Dog is to bark as _____ is to _____.

Dog is to bark as _____ is to _____.

Dog is to bark as _____ is to _____.

Dog is to bark as _____ is to _____.

For those of you whose creative muscles are feeling a bit sore, here are some likely answers.

Dog is to bark as traffic light is to flash. (a warning)
Dog is to bark as friend is to wave. (a hello)
Dog is to bark as child is to cry. (fear)

Opposites

Two and a half decades ago Dr. David Rothenberg, a psychiatrist at the Austen Riggs Center in Stockbridge, Massachusetts, was doing research on schizophrenia. As part of his battery of tests he administered a word association test to his patients. A word association test directs the test taker to respond to a stimulus word with the first word that comes to mind. The test taker is not supposed to think much about his answer, just respond with the first thing that comes to mind. What Dr. Rothenberg noticed was to gain great interest by creativity researchers and redirect the course of research in the field of creativity. A high proportion of the answers offered by his schizophrenic patients on a standardized word association test were opposites. This was especially odd as the research on word association tests shows that most people treat the stimulus word as a characteristic of something. So typical answers are *beautiful/girl, light/feather, tall/building, smooth/cheek*. On the contrary, Rothenberg's patients' responses were more along the lines of *beautiful/ugly, light/dark, tall/short, smooth/rough*. Rothenberg developed an hypothesis that highly creative people would also be more likely to generate an opposite in their responses to a word association task. Rothenberg tested his hypothesis by administering a ninety-nine item word association test to twelve Nobel Prize winners in chemistry, physics and medicine, and one hundred thirteen Yale University students. The results were very interesting. He found that the Nobel Prize winners offered the highest incidence of opposite responses. Students who were judged in a survey by their professors to be the most creative offered the next highest incidence of opposite answers. The remaining subjects were asked to do the test again and this time to try to generate an opposite response. Although they could do this, their response time was much slower than the Nobel Prize winners and the Yale students who spontaneously generated opposites. Rothenberg concluded his study by saying, "creative people demonstrate a consistent tendency to formulate opposites very rapidly and to conceptualize them simultaneously going beyond ordinary logic into the realm of the unexpected and unknown." Rothenberg also concluded that people with a potential for creativity can learn to be creative.

The Problem Finding Stage

What does it mean to have a potential for creativity? Developmental psychologist Patricia Arlin (1973) proposed that creativity is another stage of natural development, and that like Piaget's *formal operational thought* it's not to be taken for granted that all children will reach it. She called this stage the *problem finding* stage. Arlin's notion was that if all stages leading up to the problem finding stage were fully operational, the natural course of events would be for the individual to begin to seek problems rather than just react to them as they arise. Other stage theorists have shared similar notions. In his hierarchy of human needs, Abraham Maslow (1954) itemized *self-actualization* as the highest order need, arising after all other needs had been fulfilled. Maslow's hierarchy was an answer to motivation theorist Gregory Allport (1937), who argued that where infants and young children might be primarily motivated by physiological needs such as hunger and the relief of discomfort, adults' needs and motives go well beyond these basic needs. Maslow resolved this dilemma by placing both kinds of needs in his hierarchy, which is as follows:

1. Physiological Needs—food, water.
2. Safety Needs—security and safety.
3. Belongingness—love, affiliation.
4. Esteem—achievement, respect, approval.
5. Self-actualization—self-fulfillment, realization of potential, contribution.

Maslow also noted that highly creative people have a strong reality orientation, are able to easily distinguish the means from the end, and are spontaneous.

Other researchers such as Brown and Walter (1990) and Henessey (1994) also looked at the importance of problem finding in creativity. And reflecting back to the origins research mentioned in chapter four, you may recall that researchers found the most highly motivated students to have a sense of *playfulness* about their various endeavors, while others thought of similar tasks as *work*. Interestingly, Thomas (1989) observed that children tend to spontaneously seek problems, while adults do not. It is sad indeed that the young and innocent play at their work of discovering the world around them, with very little of the wherewithal to accomplish much, but by the time we have gained this we stop viewing our activities as play, and regard it merely as hard work.

On the topic of play, let's play one last game before we close this chapter and progress on to section two. In the following word association task, make it a point to generate only opposites. Don't rush yourself, but write down the first opposite you think of. Here goes.

truck   _____

hand   _____

sleep   _____

tractor   _____

closet   _____

snake   _____

boat   _____

tire   _____

pig   _____

lamp   _____

drum   _____

knee   _____

airplane   _____

elbow   _____

bandage   _____

feather   _____

empty   _____

fence   _____

accident   _____

fishing   _____

tearing   _____

grow   _____

measuring   _____

peeling   _____

sorry   _____

nice   _____

life   _____

trailer   _____

vacation   _____

movie   _____

book   _____

music   _____

star   _____

ocean   _____

mistake   _____

hairy   _____

rude   _____

absent   _____

obsessed   _____

wrinkle   _____

time   _____

watch   _____

screaming   _____

folding   _____

laughing   _____

mean   _____

holding   _____

jumping   _____

good   _____

backwards   _____

Some of them are pretty tough huh?

truck   _____

accident   _____

movie   _____

peeling   _____

time   _____

snake   _____

airplane   _____

elbow   _____

Well, as you might have expected, there's a trick to it. Yes, you can actually teach yourself to be more creative. Although some of the words really don't have an opposite, they all have attributes or functions that have an opposite. If you think of that, you can easily come up with an opposite. The first one above, for instance, *truck*, always stops people cold. *"There's no such thing as an opposite of truck. This is impossible."* Okay, fair enough, there may not be a pure opposite of truck. In fact, if we were to ask a physicist, she or he might tell us that the opposite of any matter is anti-matter. *Hum?* That would make this activity rather boring, wouldn't it? Other than anti-matter, there may not be a pure opposite of truck, so ask yourself another question entirely. What is it about a truck that makes it a truck? Yes, that's right! You can fill it with lots of stuff and move it somewhere else—stuff like dirt, and furniture and lumber, and rocks. Now we're getting someplace! So what is the opposite vehicle for moving stuff—the one which would hold the least? You've got it—*a motorcycle!* Now try the next one. What is it about an accident that makes it an accident? *It's not intentional.* So the opposite of an accident is *a plan*. We'll do one more and then I'll leave you to the rest. What is it about a movie that makes it a movie? It's staged, it's not real. So the opposite of a movie is *real life*. I think you can take it from here. Let us know if you get stuck on one. E-mail us at RAchat@aol.com and we will give you a clue. We recommend our games for a relaxing night of fun for all you moms, dads, and teachers out there. This may be how John Lennon and Paul McCartney came up with the creative and unique sound that was to become a music legend. "Hey Paul, what is it about classical music that makes it so nice?" "Why John, it's the cello, of course." *Voila!* Rock and classical meet and marry for instant mega-success.

SECTION TWO

❖ ❖

"LANGUAGE WISE" VERBAL INTELLIGENCE ACTIVITIES

This section includes the lessons that you'll be doing with your child to improve his verbal intelligence. There is no particular order of presentation for the lessons. The charts on pages 162 and 163 lay out the various areas of verbal intelligence, *vocabulary, grammar, memory, logical reasoning* and *creativity*, and list each lesson that pertains to that area of verbal intelligence. On pages 164 through 166 we've laid out activities that schools value and listed each lesson that will help prepare your child for that activity. On pages 160-161 is a list of all lessons broken down according to age appropriateness. If a lesson says six and older, for instance, it means it's appropriate for ages six through adult. Don't be fooled into thinking these lessons are too young for a struggling fourteen year old. Many skills and abilities in life are gained early and used throughout the lifespan—walking for instance.

How Do I Get Started?

Though none of the rest of this book is copyable, you are free to copy our lesson plan on page 167, or to simply use this format as a guide in designing your own lesson plans. At the Read America clinic we use a journal for each student, following the format in the lesson plan on page 148. Look over the charts on pages

162 through 166 to decide what areas you want to work on. Now look at the age appropriate chart on pages 160-161, checking what is appropriate to your child. Look these over and decide one to three lessons to work on this week. Turn to page 167 or open your journal if you're using one. Mark down the lessons you're planning on working on this week on the weekly lesson plan or in your journal. In the section *preliminary notes*, make any particular notes about the nature of your plan that you feel are relevant at this point. After you've done the lesson or lessons, mark down any relevant notes in the section *final notes*. A typical plan might look like this.

WEEKLY LESSON PLAN

Week of ___Feb.17___

Goals

Improve Bobby's ability to figure out word meanings on his own.
Improve Bobby's working vocabulary.
Work on writing something longer than a few sentences.

Lessons	Start Page
Word Detective	171
Stand Ins	196
Using Elaboration in Writing	234

Preliminary Notes

Use 'Harry Potter' as a book for practicing Word Detective after doing the lesson.
Also use sentences from 'Harry Potter' for Stand Ins after doing some of them using simple sentences.
For elaboration have Bobby describe the contents of his fishing box.

Final Notes

Use some of the Word Detective words in conversation this week.
Play Stand Ins with kids in morning car pool. Have Bobby explain how to play.
Too much stuff in fishing box for this lesson. Next week do one lure.

Should I Repeat Lessons?

Lessons should be repeated as much as you and your child like. Chances are these activities will be enjoyed by both of you and will become like old, familiar friends.

Where Should We Work?

When you first start doing these activities with your child you should be fairly formal about it. Work in a quiet place, at a table. Always sit across from your child as this helps you maintain control over the setting. By sitting across from him you can better judge when he is working or not, confused, paying attention or not, or just goofing around. As the activities become tried and true you can be much less formal about them.

The Activities as Games

Once your child has become adept at the flow of an activity you can start to play it like a game. There are lots of occasions for this in the course of your regular day. A few suggestions are: in the car on the way to school (or anywhere else), at the dinner table, while you're preparing dinner, washing dishes, folding laundry, while you're practicing or playing sports with your child, on walks, on bike rides, at the beach, canoeing, gardening. I'm sure your particular life style contains opportunities I haven't thought of. Write these down here.

_____

_____

_____

_____

Your child may also enjoy playing these games with his friends. The activities are great on a rainy day or at a slumber party. And don't be afraid to use the activities as a tradeoff, "I'll buy you that candy bar if you can tell me ten uses for the wrapper" (Brainstorming, page 228).

The Activities as Assignments

We've always given our children extra work over and above their homework assignments. They've not always been happy about it, but they've always done as they were asked. Parents tend to avoid this because they're so worried about their children doing well on their school homework assignments that they fear to overburden them with more. We take a slightly different view of this. We want our children to do well in school and in life, and we want them to be as smart as they can be. So, we give them as much work as they can manage toward these goals. In the end their school work will be easier for them if they're more intelligent. As your child becomes more capable and self-disciplined in doing the activities you can start to give them as assignments. Always do each lesson with him first though. We would not recommend that his first exposure to any lesson be in the form of an assignment.

An Assignment for You

As you've learned from this book, to know something, really *know* it, you need to make it part of your own schema. We've devised an assignment to help you do this with the *Language Wise* lessons. On pages 158-159 you'll see headings marked *Formal Lesson, Games with Me, Games with Other Children,* and *Assignments*. Look over each lesson and write it in the appropriate list or lists. Many lessons will work for in more than one of these ways.

What Do I Do When My Child's Work Contains Errors?

Remember from chapter two, mistakes are the only way we humans learn. Every mistake is an opportunity for your child to become better than he was when he made the mistake. How much better will depend upon your management of the correction. There are certain things that you'll need to help your child improve that are not mentioned directly in the lessons, but pertain to each lesson in the program. These are explained in some detail here.

Overall Meaning

Meaning is the reason for communication. It's the first thing that you want to check for in all of your child's work. It's fundamental to everything else. Most meaning based errors will turn out to be grammatically based, though some will just be nonsense. Devise questions to help the child self-correct his meaning based errors. For instance, your child is doing the lesson *Comparison and Contrast*, comparing and contrasting a pencil and a pen. He writes, "A pencil has an eraser and so they're easier to use." This question has two meaning based problems. One is grammatical and the other is a matter of clarification. A grammatical problem would be handled something like this.

You say, "You said, 'A pencil has an eraser and so they're easier to use.' Who are 'they'?"

The child says, "The pencils."

You say, "That would be 'the pencils are easier to use...'. But you said 'a pencil has an eraser,' so _____ is easier to use." Lay out a pencil in one spot on the table and a handful of pencils in another spot. Say, "Show me it." Wait for the child to indicate the pencil. Say, "Show me they."

This example is easy to correct because you can lay pencils down on the table. We keep plastic counters around for this purpose. So if for instance the child was talking about zebras you could lay down one counter and say, "This is one zebra, etc." You can also use pennies for this purpose.

If the meaning is unclear, handle it something like this.

You say, "What is it about an eraser that makes a pencil easier to use?"

The child says, "You can erase your mistakes."

You say, "Add that to your sentence please."

The child says, "A pencil has an eraser and so when you make a mistake you can erase it. That makes it easier to use a pencil than a pen."

Another kind of meaning based problem involves sequence. Sequencing problems occur because the child is thinking faster than he can write. Sequencing problems can be corrected by breaking the paragraph up into sentences and then having the child put them in the order in which they occurred.

Vocabulary

As your child begins to try his new skills he may use the wrong word from time to time in his written work. Even adults do this. A popular columnist recently poked fun at a writer who described her dog as a *bagel*. One can only assume she meant *beagle*. I recently sat in on a *Language Wise* session at the Read America clinic. Eleven year old Joe was working with Sarah, one of our therapists. Sarah was reading a piece Joe had written for a homework assignment she'd given him. It was an exercise in comparing and contrasting a candle and an electric lamp. Joe wrote, "*Hysterically*, candles were used to light houses." Of course he meant *historically*. Joe had heard both words used before, but as a child who has done very little reading until lately, he hadn't seen the words written. Sarah's correction was to say, "Were people upset when they used the candles?" "No, why are you asking me that?" Joe queried. "*Hysterically* means *upset*. I think you're thinking of a word that sounds like hysterical. Do you mean that in history people used candles?" "Yeah," answered Joe. "Alright then, hyster*ically*, histor___?" "Oh, historically!"

The fact that words sound similar is not always why they are misused. Sometimes children overgeneralize a word meaning. Seven year old Candice was attending *Language Wise* therapy after having been diagnosed as developmentally delayed two years earlier. Her vocabulary had significantly lagged behind her peers. She was asked to describe a clay vase we have in our office which was a gift from a previous client. In her description she said that the vase was *naked*. "Do you mean it hasn't got any clothes on?" her therapist asked. "No!" Candice answered looking worried. "I mean it's not a color." "Why do you suppose it isn't a color?" her therapist asked. "Nobody colored it?" Candice ventured. "That's right. What do you suppose we use to put color on things like this vase?" the therapist pressed further. "Paint?" Candice offered. "That's right Candice. So the vase is *not painted*." She wrote this on the tabletop white board in front of them. "This is two words. Another way to say *not painted* is *unpainted*." She wrote this word underneath. "*Unpainted* is just one word."

Grammar

After we've gotten all the meaning based and vocabulary based kinks out of the child's work, it's time to edit out all the grammatical errors. Here's one I saw the other day written by fourteen year old Xander, who was writing a piece entitled *Next Year*. Xander was to describe what he thought his life would be like in one year. One of the sentences in the piece read, "Sue and me want to be in the drama club." His therapist asked him, "So you want to be in the drama club do you?" "Yeah I do," he answered. "Why didn't you say 'me do' like you did here in your piece?" "It doesn't sound right," Xander answered. "It's I do," he announced with some certainty. "Yes you're right, it is 'I do'. So you should change it here. It's Sue and *I* want to be in the drama club."

Punctuation

The importance of those tiny little markings is something that remains a mystery to many children for many years. Our lesson *Exclamation Point* is a fun and very effective way of improving your child's attention to the need for punctuation and his knowledge of where to punctuate and with what marking. I find that it's very easy to get children to understand what the various markings are, but getting them to use them is much more difficult. This doesn't surprise me. Written language is merely a representation of spoken language. When we speak we don't have to stop and punctuate. Our intonation does this for us naturally. But when we write we do. We want children's writing to be a reflection of their speech. We want this to be as smooth and natural as speech is, without overburdening them with too much to think about when they write. So the goal of this lesson is to get the child used to noticing the places where the marks would be in spoken language. In this lesson you explain briefly what the markings are for. Have a piece of paper or poster board on the table with the marks you're teaching in bold marker on the paper. Ask him to point to the appropriate mark at the appropriate time. Read to the child from a book using quite a lot of intonation. Once you've played this game it becomes very easy to correct the child's work in this same way. Simply read his work to him and ask him to indicate the correct marks at the appropriate times as you read.

Spelling

You've conquered many obstacles by the time you're ready to edit your child's spelling errors. Most spelling errors that the average literate child will make will be phonetically accurate. Your child might spell the sound 'sh' in the word 'machine' as <sh> instead of <ch>, or the sound 'ee' in the word 'please' as <ee> instead of <ea>. These should be corrected appropriately. Simply indicate the <ee> and say, "This is one way to show 'ee', but there's another way that we use in this word and in other words too. Check the dictionary please." He might also have trouble with the weaker sounds in spoken language, like in the words 'ability', often spelled <abiluty>, or 'hurricane', frequently spelled <hurrucane>, or with one <r>. If your child's spelling errors contain missing or reversed sounds we suggest you obtain our book *Reading Reflex*.

Style, Content and Length

We're into more subtle turf here. You don't want your child to think you don't like his work. Be very careful as you proceed. I find that requiring length can be problematic in the sense that the child starts focusing on lots and lots of lists of things rather than on content and style. One way to improve style and content without offending the student is to use some of the *Language Wise* lessons on their written pieces as a matter of course. "Great, Sally, you've finished your piece, we've edited it for punctuation and grammar. It's pretty good. Now let's play some games with it. Here in your first sentence you've said, 'My cat is very big.' Let's take another piece of paper and write down all the words you can think of for size, in order from smallest to biggest" (*Ranking and Rating*). When she's done ask her which of these sizes best describes her cat. Now you'll end up with, 'My cat is huge.' *Language Wise* lessons that can be used in this way are: *Ranking and Rating, Word Detective, Feelings and Actions, Sets and Statements, Connections, Word Soup, Stand Ins, Word Sandwiches, Using Telling Tools, Just the Facts, Systematic Reasoning, Comparison and Contrast, Analogies, Follow That Thought, Using Meaning and Context, Using Elaboration in Writing, How-to Expository Writing, Using Inference, Resolving Logical Inconsistencies, Deduction Junction, Word Orientation, Maintaining Logic, Pros and Cons, Clarifying Ambiguity, Brainstorming, Heuristic Problem Solving, Fallacies, Exposition Using Visual Cues,* and *Interactive Writing.*

Use *Language Wise* Techniques When Your Child is Reading

Every *Language Wise* lesson can be used subtly while your child is reading in text. We strongly urge you to make these techniques part of what you do with your child when he reads so that they will in turn become part of what he does when he's reading on his own. You must do both though. Use the lessons along with the examples given in each lesson and also in text with words and sentences he's reading. Using the lessons alone establishes the formal instructional relationship between you and your child and teaches you both what the lessons are about. Using the techniques from the lessons when your child is reading makes them automatic for him and bridges the gap to real world application. We'll use excerpts from one of the new *Harry Potter* (J.K. Rowling, Bloomsbury) books to offer examples of using *Language Wise* techniques while doing text reading.

Question for Understanding Based on Memory

> Mrs Weasley fussed over the state of his socks and tried to force him to eat fourth helpings at every meal.

When your child is reading to you think of questions that check for his memory of what he read. A few sentences after a detail has been mentioned, just phrase a question that checks your child's memory of the detail. So in the above example you might wait until the end of the paragraph to ask, "So what did Mrs. Weasley fuss about?"

Question for Understanding Based on Inference

Ask questions that check that your child is making inferences that allow him to build meaning as he goes. So you might ask your child, "Why do you suppose Mrs. Weasley fussed about Harry's socks?" If he makes an incorrect inference, "She didn't like him much," move to the portion of the text that reveals the answer.

> *What Harry found most unusual about life at Ron's, however, wasn't the talking mirror or the clanking ghoul: it was the fact that everybody there seemed to like him.*

Question for Understanding Based on Logical Reasoning

Set up little traps to catch your child and test his logical reasoning. Remember, if he doesn't make errors he won't learn.

> *Hagrid seized Harry by the scruff of the neck and pulled him away from the witch, knocking the tray right out of her hands. Her shrieks followed them along the twisting alleyway out into bright sunlight.*

Using this example above ask, "So where is the witch now?" If he answers, "Following Harry and Hagrid," say, "Read the second sentence please." After he has done so ask, "Tell me the words that say what followed." He should say, "Her shrieks followed."

Question to Check Your Child's Ability to Understand Figurative Usage

When figurative language appears in text ask a question that allows your child to make an error about the meaning. This will reveal whether he really understands the meaning of the usage.

> *Harry fought to keep his face straight as he emerged.*

Using this example ask, "So was Harry fighting?" Your child should explain that it was only a struggle with himself, not to laugh. Take these opportunities to teach your child the term *figurative*.

Question to Check Your Child's Ability to Find Word Meanings Based on Context

Question your child to be certain that he's using context to figure out what new words mean.

> She <u>leered</u> at him, showing mossy teeth. Harry backed away.

In this example ask what *leered* means. If he doesn't know, ask what one might be doing if their teeth were showing. If he answers to say, "smiling," ask if Harry would back away if she was smiling.

Question Your Child's Ability to Think Creatively about the Story

Seek out and use opportunities to let your child think creatively about the story as he reads it.

> Harry Potter was a wizard—a wizard fresh from his first year at Hogwarts School of Witchcraft and Wizardry. And if the Dursleys were unhappy to have him back for the holidays, it was nothing to how Harry felt.

In this example ask questions on the topic of why the Dursleys (Harry's Aunt and Uncle) might not like having him around. Ask your child what he thinks it might be like to have a wizard living in your house, or what it might be like to *be* a wizard.

Question for Your Child's Ability to Use Analogies to Understand the Story

Invite your child to make analogies from his own life in order to understand the story.

> He gazed miserably into the hedge. He had never felt so lonely. Harry missed his best friends, Ron Weasley and Hermione Granger. They, however, didn't seem to be missing him at all. Neither of them had written to him all summer, even though Ron had said he was going to ask Harry to come and stay.

In this example ask questions that cause your child to make analogies. "Do you recall a time when you were sad for a similar reason to Harry?"

Look through the lessons and determine which would be best for my child as formal lessons, which would work well as games to be played with me, which would work well as games to be played with other children, and which would work as assignments.

Formal Lessons   Games with Me

_____   _____

_____   _____

_____   _____

_____   _____

_____   _____

_____   _____

_____   _____

_____   _____

_____   _____

_____   _____

_____   _____

_____   _____

_____   _____

_____   _____

_____   _____

_____   _____

_____   _____

_____   _____

_____   _____

_____   _____

Games with Other Children

_____
_____
_____
_____
_____
_____
_____
_____
_____
_____
_____
_____
_____
_____
_____
_____
_____
_____
_____
_____

Assignments

_____
_____
_____
_____
_____
_____
_____
_____
_____
_____
_____
_____
_____
_____
_____
_____
_____
_____
_____
_____

LESSONS BY AGES

Lessons for Eight Years Old to Adult

Lessons for Nine Years Old to Adult

APPLICATION OF LESSONS TO VERBAL INTELLIGENCE

Vocabulary

Ranking and Rating

Word Detective

Feelings and Actions

Guess What

Sets and Statements

Connections

Word Soup

Using Opposites

Stand Ins

Comparison and Contrast

Analogies

Caveman Game

Understanding Telling Tools

Telling Tools

Using Telling Tools

Pros and Cons

Using Meaning and Context

Clarifying Ambiguity

Brainstorming

Using Elaboration in Writing

How-To Expository Writing

Using Inference

Exposition Using Visual Cues

Resolving Logical Inconsistencies

Deduction Junction

Word Sandwiches

Word Orientation

Memory

Ranking and Rating

Guess What

Sets and Statements

Word Soup

Connections

Operating on Memory

Building on Memory

Comparison and Contrast

Follow That Thought

Using Elaboration in Writing

How-To Expository Writing

Using Inference

Exposition Using Visual Cues

Deduction Junction

Grammar

Word Detective

Guess What

Sets and Statements

Connections

Word Soup

Using Opposites

Stand Ins

Maintaining Logic

Systematic Reasoning

Comparison and Contrast

Follow That Thought

Caveman Game

Understanding Telling Tools

Telling Tools

Using Telling Tools

Using Meaning and Context

Clarifying Ambiguity

Fallacies

Using Elaboration in Writing

How-To Expository Writing

Using Inference

Exposition Using Visual Cues

Resolving Logical Inconsistencies

Deduction Junction

Word Sandwiches

Fast Talk

Exclamation Point!

Logical Reasoning

Ranking and Rating
Word Detective
Feelings and Actions
Guess What
Sets and Statements
Connections
Using Opposites
Operating on Memory
Building on Memory
Stand Ins
Maintaining Logic
Systematic Reasoning
Comparison and Contrast
Analogies
Follow That Thought
Caveman Game
Understanding Telling Tools
Telling Tools
Using Telling Tools
Pros and Cons
Using Meaning and Context
Clarifying Ambiguity
Brainstorming
Heuristic Problem Solving
Fallacies
How-To Expository Writing
Using Elaboration in Writing
Using Inference
Exposition Using Visual Cues
Resolving Logical Inconsistencies
Deduction Junction
Word Sandwiches
Just the Facts
Word Orientation

Creativity

Word Detective
Feelings and Actions
Guess What
Sets and Statements
Connections
Word Soup
Using Opposites
Stand Ins
Systematic Reasoning
Comparison and Contrast
Analogies
Caveman Game
Understanding Telling Tools
Telling Tools
Using Telling Tools
Pros and Cons
Using Meaning and Context
Clarifying Ambiguity
Brainstorming
Heuristic Problem Solving
Fallacies
Using Elaboration in Writing
Using Inference
Exposition Using Visual Cues
Resolving Logical Inconsistencies
Deduction Junction
Word Sandwiches
Word Orientation
Maintaining Logic

APPLICATION OF LESSONS TO SCHOOL ASSIGNMENTS

Journal Writing

Caveman Game
Stand Ins
Maintaining Logic
Sets and Statements
Feelings & Actions
Word Soup
Word Sandwiches
Using Opposites
Follow That Thought
Resolving Logical Inconsistencies
Deduction Junction
Clarifying Ambiguity
Just the Facts
Using Meaning & Context
Fallacies
Fast Talk
Using Elaboration in Writing
Understanding Telling Tools
Telling Tools
Using Telling Tools
Interactive Writing
Word Sandwiches
Interactive Writing
Exclamation Point!

Aural Skills

Caveman Game
Stand Ins
Maintaining Logic
Sets and Statements
Systematic Reasoning
Guess What
Connections
Feelings & Actions
Word Soup
Word Sandwiches
Using Opposites
Word Detective
Operating on Memory
Building on Memory
Follow That Thought
Resolving Logical Inconsistencies
Deduction Junction
Clarifying Ambiguity
Just the Facts
Using Inferences
Using Meaning & Context
Heuristic Problem Solving
Fallacies
Brainstorming
Using Elaboration in Writing
Interactive Writing
Understanding Telling Tools
Telling Tools
Using Telling Tools
Using Visual Cues
Fast Talk
Word Orientation

Fiction Reading & Writing

Caveman Game
Stand Ins
Maintaining Logic
Sets and Statements
Systematic Reasoning
Guess What
Connections
Feelings & Actions
Word Soup
Word Sandwiches
Using Opposites
Word Detective
Operating on Memory
Building on Memory
Follow That Thought
Resolving Logical Inconsistencies
Deduction Junction
Clarifying Ambiguity
Just the Facts
Using Inferences
Using Meaning & Context
Heuristic Problem Solving
Fallacies
Brainstorming
Using Elaboration in Writing
Interactive Writing
Understanding Telling Tools
Telling Tools
Using Telling Tools
Using Visual Cues
Just the Facts
Word Orientation
Exclamation Point!

Autobiographical & Biographical Reading & Writing

Caveman Game
Stand Ins
Maintaining Logic
Sets and Statements
Systematic Reasoning
Connections
Word Soup
Word Detective
Operating on Memory
Building on Memory
Follow That Thought
Resolving Logical Inconsistencies
Deduction Junction
Clarifying Ambiguity
Just the Facts
Using Inference
Using Meaning & Context
Heuristic Problem Solving
Fallacies
Using Elaboration in Writing
Interactive Writing
Understanding Telling Tools
Telling Tools
Using Telling Tools
Comparison & Contrast
Just the Facts
Word Orientation
Exclamation Point!

Writing Summaries

Caveman Game

Stand Ins

Maintaining Logic

Sets and Statements

Systematic Reasoning

Word Sandwiches

Follow That Thought

Resolving Logical Inconsistencies

Deduction Junction

Clarifying Ambiguity

Just the Facts

Using Inferences

Using Meaning & Context

Heuristic Problem Solving

Fast Talk

How-To Expository Writing

Understanding Telling Tools

Telling Tools

Using Telling Tools

Pros & Cons

Just the Facts

Fast Talk

Interactive Writing

Exclamation Point!

Writing Book Reports

Caveman Game

Stand Ins

Maintaining Logic

Sets and Statements

Systematic Reasoning

Word Detective

Follow That Thought

Resolving Logical Inconsistencies

Deduction Junction

Clarifying Ambiguity

Just the Facts

Using Inference

Using Meaning & Context

Heuristic Problem Solving

How-To Expository Writing

Interactive Writing

Understanding Telling Tools

Telling Tools

Using Telling Tools

Comparison & Contrast

Word Sandwiches

Interactive Writing

Exclamation Point!

Writing Comparison & Contrast

Caveman Game

Stand Ins

Maintaining Logic

Sets & Statements

Comparison & Contrast

Sets and Statements

Systematic Reasoning

Guess What

Connections

Word Soup

Follow That Thought

Deduction Junction

Clarifying Ambiguity

Just the Facts

Using Inferences

Using Meaning & Context

Heuristic Problem Solving

Fast Talk

Using Elaboration

Understanding Telling Tools

Telling Tools

Using Telling Tools

Pros & Cons

Interactive Writing

WEEKLY LESSON PLAN

Week of _____

Goals

_____
_____
_____
_____
_____

Lessons   Start Page

_____   _____
_____   _____
_____   _____

Preliminary Notes

_____
_____
_____
_____
_____

Final Notes

_____
_____
_____
_____
_____
_____
_____

RANKING AND RATING

Goals

To offer the child experience at making sequenced or graded determinations.

Improves

vocabulary

memory

logical reasoning

Age Appropriateness

Five years and older.

Materials

If you are working with a young child you may need some household objects (such as the items mentioned in the examples) to help the child understand the lesson. Older children should be able to imagine these items.

You will also need some paper and a pencil.

Presentation

1. Ask the child what his favorite color is. Write it down on a piece of paper. Now ask him what his least favorite color is. Write it down to the far right of his favorite color. Now ask him what his second favorite color is. Invite him to show you where to write it.

2. After you have several colors written in rank, invite the child to tell you words to describe what you have. EX: good, better, better, best

3. Now choose a concept to rank, such as size. Ask the child to tell you a word to describe it. EX: little Invite the child to tell you where it should go on the list. Continue to question him to get him to generate as many words as he can to describe size, writing each on the list in the appropriate place. Your list may look something like this:

tiny—small—little—average—big—large—giant—huge

4. When he's done, take the opportunity to teach him some new words to describe size.

infinitesimal, minuscule, gargantuan, enormous, vast

List of Concepts to Rank

moods ⎯⎯⎯⎯⎯⎯⎯⎯⎯⎯⎯→

texture

temperature

weight

wetness

light to dark

level of difficulty

tightness

degrees of hunger

degrees of tiredness

degrees of thirst

coolness

emotions

height

relationships

friendliness

intelligence

speed

agility

depth

distance

<u>moods</u>

ecstatic
elated
happy
content
mellow
indifferent
sad
miserable
depressed
devastated

age

fragrance

beauty

frequency

enthusiasm

purpose

wealth

flexibility

brokenness

weirdness

personality

quality

achievement

WORD DETECTIVE

Goals

This activity will help the child learn to build a strategy for figuring out what words mean based on the context of the sentence in which they occur.

This activity will help the child learn to build a strategy of questioning that will enable her to discover the meaning of a word when the existing information is not sufficient.

Improves

vocabulary

grammar

logical reasoning

creativity

Age Appropriateness

This activity is appropriate for a mature six year old and older. The challenge is finding vocabulary that is appropriate. Experimentation may be necessary.

Materials

You'll need a good age appropriate dictionary for reference during this lesson. We suggest *Webster's Elementary Dictionary*. Although it presents itself as an elementary grades dictionary, it contains numerous entries of words that the average middle school child doesn't know. In all it has 32,000 entries. If you're dealing with a precocious child you might want to use a good unabridged dictionary. You might even learn a few new words yourself.

You will also need some paper and a pencil.

Presentation

1. Tell the child that you're going to play a word detective game. Tell her the game will teach her new words. Explain that you are going to say a sentence and in it will be the word you want her to figure out. Tell her she can figure out

the word by using the sentence it's in. Explain that you are going to start with a made-up word for practice.

2. Tell her the word is **'smup'**. Say, "The **smup** barked at the mail man." (dog) Continue on with these practice sentences.

"We went on a **smittle** in the country." Explain that she needs more information. Say, "We went on a **smittle** in the country. We brought a blanket and a **smittle** basket." (picnic)

"I like plomet." Discuss the fact that she can't exactly tell what **plomet** is. It could be anything she likes. Explain that she needs more information. Say, "I like plomet. My teacher is very nice." (school)

3. Say, "Now we are going to use a real word that you don't know." The following is a short list of suggested vocabulary words with sample sentences. These will get you started and give you some examples of sentences that reveal meaning.

The man with the red polka-dot jacket, boots and a skirt looked **absurd**.

The bird was **aloft** among the clouds.

I'm going to give you two **alternatives**. You can go straight to bed or you can behave.

I want to **eradicate** the ants from this house.

My friends **deluded** me into thinking they had forgotten my birthday. But they gave me a surprise party.

The mountain climber was very tired, but he knew he must **persevere** if he was to reach the top of the mountain.

Oranges are the **origin** of orange juice.

The mailman brought me a **parcel** with a gift in it.

The car **obscured** my view of the robbery, so I wasn't able to describe the burglar.

I was **perplexed** to find an apple growing on an orange tree.

Refrain from jumping on the couch or you'll be in big trouble.

4. Now offer the child some practice figuring out what questions to ask when a sentence or two doesn't provide enough context information to unlock the word meaning. Warn her that these are a little harder. *Aren't you **venturesome** today.* Say, "Why can't you figure out what **venturesome** means? What's the problem?" Your child should say something like, **Venturesome** could be anything 'you' are today." Say, "That's right, so we need to know what 'you' did to get the speaker to say she or he was **venturesome**. Well, 'you' climbed all the way to the top of a big oak tree to rescue a kitten that was stuck up there. What do you think someone is who climbs all the way to the top of a tree?" The child should say something like "brave."

Say, "That's right, and what you needed to know to figure that word out was what the person had done, what action he had taken to be called **venturesome**. Now we're going to try another one. *That's a **vibrant** color.* This one is different. The color can't do anything. Colors can't move or show action. What do you think would help you figure out what **vibrant** means?" The child should say that seeing the color would help. When you elicit this answer, show her a very vibrant color. She will probably say that vibrant means bright.

FEELINGS AND ACTIONS

Goals

To offer experience at building meaning from a state of being to a verb.

To offer experience surmising the state of being based on the action.

Age Appropriateness

Six and older.

Improves

> vocabulary
>
> logical reasoning
>
> creativity

Presentation

1. Tell the child you're going to provide a word and he should think of something you would do if you felt that way

States of Being

> sad   ⟶   cry
>
> happy
>
> mad
>
> lonely
>
> afraid
>
> tired
>
> hungry
>
> confused
>
> itchy
>
> sticky
>
> hot
>
> gone
>
> cold
>
> sick

excited
upset
jealous
whiny
cranky
stupid
embarrassed
smart
proud
anxious
hateful
overwhelmed
loving
strong
lost
dizzy
awful
goofy

Actions

smile —————————————→ happy

vomit
leave
cry
laugh
drink
clap
eat
shout
whisper

jump
sleep
sink

GUESS WHAT

Goals

To teach the child the benefits of elaboration.

To teach the child to delay the "leap to closure."

Age Appropriateness
Six and older.

Improves
vocabulary

grammar

memory

logical reasoning

creativity

Presentation

1. Explain that you're going to play a guessing game. First it's the teacher's turn. You'll describe something to the child. Do not try to reveal the item too soon. Start with subtle clues. As you offer clues have the child write down a list of what he thinks it might be. But, he shouldn't say it aloud until he's sure. Write the item down and place it in the mystery envelope.

2. He'll get ten points for a correct answer spoken aloud and he'll get one point for every guess he writes on his paper. Discuss how the scoring system encourages him to put lots of stuff on the paper and to delay his guess aloud.

3. Take turns and keep score. After each correct guess discuss what the most telling details were.

List of Items

coffee cup ──────────────▶

specific person

shower cap

bicycle

hairbrush

staple

whistle

flower

ruler

computer mouse

basketball ──────────────▶

hairdryer

phone

pager

toothbrush

cloud

wheelchair

roof

watch

tire

skateboard

window

mirror

fireworks

ear

tattoo

nose

light

earring

silence

<u>coffee cup clues</u>

I like hot stuff.

My ancestors come from China.

I'll give you a handle in the morning.

Sometimes I get invited to tea.

Without me you'd make a real mess.

I get washed every day.

<u>basketball clues</u>

I have my ups and downs.

I appear in court.

People shoot me.

You can find me in a store.

I can make points.

I like Mike.

pain
sadness
fear
jealousy
hope
joy
anger
space
book
knowledge
fact
fiction
opinion
truth
blueprint
eraser
picture frame
friend
glasses
heart
water
heat
a specific color
insult
whiteout
a post-it
a specific shape

SETS & STATEMENTS

Goals

To give the child experience organizing information into sets and forming statements about them.

Age Appropriateness

Six and older.

Improves

vocabulary

grammar

memory

logical reasoning

creativity

Materials

If you are working with a young child you may need some household objects (such as the items mentioned in the examples) to help the child understand the lesson. Older children should be able to imagine these items.

You will also need paper and a pencil.

Presentation

1. Show the child a list of items. EX: bananas, oranges, pork chops, watermelon.

2. Ask him which of these go together and which isn't part of that set.

3. Invite him to make a statement about that. EX: Bananas, oranges and watermelon are fruit. Pork chops are meat, not fruit.

4. Continue with several lists.

List of Sets

rain, sand, snow, wind

red, pink, grass, blue

dogs, elephants, earthquakes, lions

dimes, quarters, nickels, dollars

candle, match, light switch, bulb

car, bike, wagon, truck

up, down, left, north

irons, woods, putters, greens

bluebirds, flies, airplanes, geese

teeth, lips, tongue, face

goose bumps, pimples, mosquito bites, freckles

can openers, keys, corkscrew, hammer

Taco Bell, Burger King, McDonald's, Denny's

rubber bands, staples, paper clips, pencil sharpener

glasses, telescope, window, mirror

radio, TV, CD player, internet

cash, credit card, stamp, check

playing cards, baseball cards, credit cards, postcards

policeman, doctors, teachers, taxman

Post-its, thumbtacks, stamps, glue

pond, pool, lake, river

football, basketball, soccer, baseball

principal, student, counselor, teacher

poem, play, novel, biography

name, street, city, zip code

in, out, up, down

CONNECTIONS

Goals

To cause the student to establish connections when the relatedness of the word is not easily perceivable.

Age Appropriateness

Five and older

Improves

vocabulary

grammar

memory

logical reasoning

creativity

Materials

Pairs of words that have at least one thing in common

Example: smile—hear: People smile when they hear a joke.

cat—dog

tall—heavy

milk—cheese

bacon—chair

flute—stapler

blue—Oregon

lion—paper

toothpick—paint

violin—bird

dish—moon

teacher—fish

newspaper—kerosene

spoon—hair spray

sparkplug—rubber band

Arkansas—bagpipes

These are examples of answers offered by *Language Wise* students:

cat—dog	*Bobby (9) They both have fleas.* *Sarah (11) They both go to the vet.* *Alice (6) They don't come in blue.*
newspaper—kerosene	*Sarah (11) You can start fires with* *them.* *Stella (8) You can read them.* *Brinnea (18) They both have a* *bad smell.*
spoon—hair spray	*Jason (13) WalMart sells them* *both.*
sparkplug—rubber band	*Alice (6) My dad has them both in* *his toolbox.* *Bobby (9) They can make* *airplanes go.*
Arkansas—bagpipes	*David (12) They both have pipes.* *Alice (6) They both have bags.*

Presentation

1. Explain to the child that you're going to play a word game. Tell him two simple words such as cat-dog and ask him to think of a way that they are related.

2. Continue with some more word pairs.

3. Base the difficulty of your pairs on the child's success at creating categories. Each time you play the game increase the difficulty just a little bit.

List of Items

field—underwear
tooth—nail
phone—floor
socks—wind
books—water
fantasy—reality
gravel—cheese
school—eye
girls—money
barbershop—noses
chairs—chins
war—peace
shoes—coffee
stars—stripes
rain—pain
oranges—frogs
time—silence
chase—happiness
divorce—love
sound—motion
tap—balance
smoke—concrete
baby—United States
poem—cloud
frog—butterfly

dream—reality
rose—heart
morning—death
ocean—land
snow—gift
home—carnival
eggs—beach
candy—hose
Tuesday—foot
cow—bricks
garbage—cabbage
lunch—toys
dogs—carpet
cats—school
sparkplugs—milk
life—death
laughing—life
homework—chocolate
doughnuts—garbage bags
computers—books
liberty—dogs
profession—hobby
sympathy—irrelevant
grass—wine
golf—TV
enthusiasm—industriousness
thoughtfulness—effectiveness

Alternative Presentation

1. Every now and then you can let the student have a try at baffling you with a
   word pair to associate.

WORD SOUP

Goals

To help the child understand the symbolic nature of words and see that they stimulate certain related thoughts and ideas.

To give her practice making creative links to words.

To offer her practice at talking about words and the relationship between words. The kinds of relationships your prompts will inspire are:

Examples of Response Types

compound completion

truck /stop

something that uses or has the noun

tractor /farmer

something that does the verb

grow /plant

something that the noun did or had done to it

snake /hiss

someone or something that you did the verb to

empty /trash

another name for the verb or noun

boat /ship

an opposite of the verb or noun

empty /full

a categorization, a part of the prompt or the prompt as a part of the response

tire /car

an attribute that is permanent
knee /bend

a state of being
knee /hurt

Age Appropriateness

This activity is appropriate for children age six and older.

Improves

vocabulary

grammar

memory

logical reasoning

creativity

Materials

No special materials are necessary for this activity.

Presentation

1. Tell your child you're going to play a word game. Tell her that you'll say a word and she should say what it makes her think of. Tell her her answer should be only one word.

2. Say each of the words and have her offer a response.

truck   _____

hand   _____

sleep _____

tractor _____

closet _____

snake _____

boat _____

tire _____

pig _____

lamp _____

drum _____

knee _____

airplane _____

elbow _____

bandage _____

feather _____

empty _____

fence _____

accident _____

fishing _____

tearing _____

grow _____

measuring _____

peeling _____

sorry _____

nice _____

life _____

trailer _____

vacation _____

movie _____

book _____

music _____

star _____

ocean _____

mistake   _____

hairy   _____

rude   _____

absent   _____

obsessed   _____

wrinkle   _____

time   _____

watch   _____

screaming   _____

folding   _____

laughing   _____

mean   _____

holding   _____

jumping   _____

good   _____

backwards   _____

3. Ask her to tell you why she gave that answer. For example if she said 'grow/plant', she might go on to explain that plants grow. If she said 'empty/trash', she might go on to explain that Dad empties the trash.

4. Ask her to think of another kind of association (see response types).

USING OPPOSITES

Goal

This lesson gives the child an opportunity to see that even things that are the opposite of one another have mutual characteristics.

Frequently the child will choose the opposite based on form and then the similarity based on function, or vice versa. This offers an opportunity for discussion.

Age Appropriateness

Seven and older.

Improves

vocabulary

grammar

logical reasoning

creativity

Materials

You will need paper and pencil for the student to record his answers.

Presentation

1. Invite the child to tell you the opposite of some of the items on the list.

2. Now go back and invite the child to tell you something the opposites have in common. (EX) They both appear on a newspaper. If he provides the classification (EX: They are both colors), accept it as an answer, but ask if he can think of another thing they have in common. Have him formulate a sentence to state his answer. (EX) Black and white are colors that appear on a newspaper.

List of Items

big

grass

men

hair

girl

hot

winter

short

sad

work

sky

up

over

dark

motion

cry

freeze

sick

last

good

shrink

dry

leave

angry

lazy

amazing

feet

plug

travel

towel

smoke

belt

you

tree

mountain

OPERATING ON MEMORY

Goals

To give the child practice at using systematic organization and elaboration to improve on memory.

To show the child that connections are more valuable than arbitrary lists.

Age Appropriateness

Eight and older

Improves

logical reasoning

memory

Presentation

1. Ask the child how good his memory is. After he tells you what he thinks, tell him to try to remember a list of words. Tell him the words. Now ask him what the words were.

2. Now tell him that you're going to teach him some tricks to remember things. Invite him to sort the words into groups. Ask him what words might go well together. Make a list of the groups. Ask the child to explain the groups to you. (EX) These things all go in the kitchen and these things all go in the bathroom, and these things all go in the living room.

3. Now ask him to recall all the words.

4. Now ask him to write (or dictate to you) a paragraph using all the words. After he has completed this and reread it to you invite him to recall all the words.

5. Discuss how understanding the relationships between words can help you recall information. Use examples of school material that you may recall better

if you understand the 'story' between the words. History works as a good example of this. Other examples might be:

chair, floor, toothpaste, brush, dish, window, fork, TV, mirror

Example of how the child might categorize the above:

things in a bathroom—toothpaste, brush, mirror
things in a living room—TV, chair

Create a list of things from the following as in the above for use in your lessons. Some suggestions are:

things at the beach

things in the woods

things in your room

sports teams

things in a movie theater

rock bands

parts of a house

athletic shoes

designer clothes

magazines

makeup

kinds of breakfast cereal

kinds of desserts

bodies of water

types of transportation

emotions

a list of names

BUILDING ON MEMORY

Goals

To cause the student to realize the nature of recognition and recall. To offer him a strategy for recalling what he doesn't recognize, and for moving information from recall memory to recognition memory.

Age Appropriateness

Seven and older

Improves

logical reasoning

memory

Materials

Telephone numbers, addresses, vocabulary words, names and paragraphs containing information that is familiar to the child, and information that is new to the child.

Presentation

1. Explain to the child that there are two different kinds of remembering. Explain that we remember, for instance, the names of our friends without having to try, but when we meet new people, we have to *try* to remember their names.

2. Invite the child to play a game of remembering with you. Ask him to tell you the names of three of his friends. For the purposes of this example let's say he told you Joey, Tim and Patrick. Now say, "Great, I'm going to add two new people to your group, Sandy and George. Now, if I ask you to tell me all the names in a few minutes, you can remember your friends' names without trying, but you will have to try to remember the two new ones."

3. Chat casually with the child for a few minutes about something else to allow some time to pass. Then say, "Can you remember all the names I asked you to remember?" If he offers all the names with accuracy, point out that it was easy, because all he really had to work at were the two new ones. If he can't

supply the names, remind him of what it is he has to work at... the two new names. Ask if he can remember them. Once he does, ask him to tell you the names of his three friends.

4. Practice some more with the child. Ask him his phone number. For the purposes of this example let's say he said 492-8739. Say, "Great, I'm going to give you another phone number to remember. It is 492-4418. Do you have to work at remembering the whole number?" Direct him as needed to realize that the first three numbers are the same as his phone number and so all he needs to remember are the last four.

5. Continue practice with other examples. You can use vocabulary words, names, phone numbers and addresses.

6. As you practice this activity with the child, and he begins to demonstrate that he understands the issues, introduce paragraphs of information to him. After reading one such paragraph, ask him to itemize what he already knows, and doesn't have to remember, and what is new information to him. Ask him to try to remember the new information until your next session. At the next session, quiz him about the new and the old information together.

STAND INS

Goals

To offer practice at generating possible words to use in spoken and written language.

Age Appropriateness

Six and older. Note: Six and seven year olds may do best if asked to change only one word in a sentence.

Improves

> vocabulary
>
> grammar
>
> logical reasoning
>
> creativity

Presentation

1. Tell the child a sentence and invite him to think of all the words he can to replace a target word/s without changing the meaning.

List of Sentences

> The cat was <u>big</u>.
>
> The dog barked <u>noisily</u>.
>
> Dinner was <u>tasty</u>.
>
> John ran <u>quickly</u>.
>
> The tree was <u>tall</u>.
>
> The pizza was <u>mushy</u>.
>
> The ride was <u>exciting</u>.
>
> My mother is <u>kind</u>.
>
> The car went <u>fast</u>.
>
> The <u>brown</u> dog ran <u>quickly</u> to the <u>big</u> house.

The <u>girl</u> was <u>beautiful</u>.

Her <u>jeans</u> were too <u>tight</u>.

The <u>motorcycle</u> was <u>loud</u>.

The red <u>car</u> <u>raced</u> past.

The <u>surf</u> is <u>choppy</u>.

The voices of the <u>angry</u> children <u>echoed</u> loudly in the empty <u>hall</u>.

Use sentences from books the child is reading when you've exhausted this list of examples.

MAINTAINING LOGIC

Goals

To offer the child practice at maintaining internal consistency in his writing.

Age Appropriateness

Mature eight or older. The child should have completed the lesson Stand Ins.

Improves

    grammar

    logical reasoning

    creativity

Presentation

1. Offer the child a passage from a story or informative piece.

2. Explain that his job is to change all the nouns without changing the meaning of the story.

3. Now have him change all the verbs.

4. Now have him change all the describing words.

   He will discover that some things can't be changed and maintain the meaning—such as numbers.

SYSTEMATIC REASONING

Goals

Offer the child practice at solving classification problems through systematic reasoning.

Offer the child experiences forming sets and super sets.

Age Appropriateness

Eight or older.

Improves

grammar

logical reasoning

creativity

Materials

Household items and things in nature for consideration.

Presentation

1. Using the following examples and others you generate on your own, ask the child the question.

2. Ask the child to tell you what criteria he or she has based the answer on.

3. Ask the child if the criterion is one of form or function.

List of Questions

Is a stool more like a chair or a sofa?

Is Jell-O more like ice cream or Kool Aid?

Is Christmas more like Thanksgiving or Easter?

Is a girl more like a boy or a woman?

Is a baby more like a child or a puppy?

Is a bush more like a tree or a flower?

Is a cake more like bread or candy?

Is snowboarding more like surfing or swimming?

Is juice more like fruit or water?

Is reading more like writing or speaking?

Is love more like hope or peace?

Is a clock more like a watch or time?

Is paper more like a tree or leather?

Is money more like food or guns?

Is survival more like skill or luck?

Is a leaf more like hair or a flower?

Is a bird more like a fish or an airplane?

Is a teacher more like a friend or a mother?

Is a school more like a prison or a sanctuary?

Is a cushion more like a chair or a pillow?

Is a doorknob more like a ball or a handle?

Is an eye more like a mirror, a window, or a camera?

Is a paper clip more like a staple or a clothespin?

Is a flag more like a sign or a letter?

Is a boat more like a plane or a train?

Is a boy more like a father or a brother?

Is a shoe more like a glove or a sweater?

Is a slipper more like a shoe or a sock?

Am I more like myself or me?

Is a vet more like a farmer or a doctor?

Is a truck more like a bus or a car?

Is a book more like a picture or a story?

Is a wall more like a floor or a ceiling?

Is a window more like a door or a wall?

Is a bridge more like a road or a rainbow?

Is a snack more like lunch or breakfast?

Is a snake more like a lizard or an eel?

Is a shell more like a nest or a house?

Is an ocean more like a pond or a river?

Is a sky more like a fact or a possibility?

Is a belief more like a cage or space?

Is a cloud more like water or air?

COMPARISON & CONTRAST

Goals

To offer the child practice at making connections between two things or concepts.

Age Appropriateness

Eight and older.

Improves

vocabulary

grammar

memory

logical reasoning

creativity

Presentation

1. Explain that sometimes you need to be able to think about how things are alike or not alike—how they 'compare and contrast'.

2. Choose one of the pairs from the list. Draw two overlapping circles on a piece of paper.

   Label each circle as one of the items you're comparing and contrasting. Choosing one to start with, begin to list its attributes and functions. Whenever you come upon an attribute or function that is also true of the other, list it in the interlocking area. Each of you can offer input.

3. Have him write about how the items compare and contrast in each of these topics. His piece should contain a paragraph on each item with comparison and contrast.

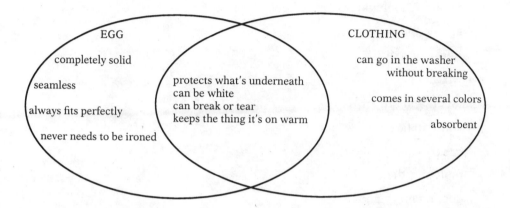

EGG
completely solid
seamless
always fits perfectly
never needs to be ironed

protects what's underneath
can be white
can break or tear
keeps the thing it's on warm

CLOTHING
can go in the washer
without breaking
comes in several colors
absorbent

List of Things to Compare and Contrast

an egg and clothing

a book and a movie on video

a pencil and a pen

paper and a keyboard

poetry and prose

television and the internet

reading and writing

school and a job

hearing and listening

whispering and screaming

understanding and confusion

an eyelid and the shutter on a camera

eyeshadow and paint

any two countries

any two cities

any two states

public school and private school

create and destroy

infuse and distill

whiteout and eraser

lunch and dinner

stiff and flexible

car trip and plane trip

molt and shed

documentary and movie

cats and dogs

birds and chickens

birds and dinosaurs

letter and e-mail

telephone and letter

ocean and space

telephone and a face to face conversation

ocean and space

glovebox and shoe box

ANALOGIES

Goals

To offer the child practice at understanding the logical structure of an
analogy.

Age Appropriateness

Eight or older. The child should complete the lesson Systematic Reasoning before doing this lesson.

Improves

vocabulary

logical reasoning

creativity

Presentation

1. Explain to the child that analogies are a way of teaching something or illustrating a point. Explain that you want him to see what you mean so you're
going to make up a pretend word, 'smiz', and then show him how he can figure out what it means by using an analogy.

2. Now say, "OK—a 'smiz' is to flying as a boy is to walking."

3. Move to the examples, inviting the child to solve each one.

4. Invite the child to develop some analogies of his own.

List of Analogies

girl is to walks as eagle is to

six is to three as eight is to

in is to out as on is to

he is to man as she is to

mom is to dad as sister is to

green is to go as red is to

rainfall is to summer as snowfall is to

pizza is to eat as book is to

game is to play as work is to

quack is to duck as bark is to

twelve is to ten as four is to

finger is to hand as toe is to

apple is to red as cucumber is to

Mr. is to gentleman as Mrs. is to

drive is to boat as fly is to

listen is to CD as watch is to

taste is to mouth as smell is to

floor is to carpet as table is to

desert is to dry as lake is to

dog is to fur as fish is to

valley is to low as mountain is to

legal is to right as illegal is to

picture is to draw as book is to

peace is to agree as war is to

chapter is to a book as act is to a

weld is to metal as glue is to

boat is to camel as car is to

fingers are to piano as mouth is to

pink is to red as grey is to

salt is to shaker as milk is to

trio is to three as duet is to

author is to book as composer is to

town is to county as state is to

gobble is to nibble as gulp is to

scalpel is to doctor as paintbrush is to

Shakespeare is to plays as Elton John is to

eskimo is to kayak as canoe is to

machine is to patent as book is to

speedometer is to speed as altimeter is to

admiral is to navy as general is to

meat is to carnivore as plants are to

country is to rural as city is to

unimportant is to important as tiny is to

Jesus is to parable as Aesop is to

textile is to loom as photograph is to

abstinence is to moderation as none is to

aged is to geriatrics as child is to

sphere is to circle as cube is to

FOLLOW THAT THOUGHT

Goals

To give the child practice at distinguishing between object and subject in unusually stated but valid sentences.

To give the child practice at restating statements by moving the subject and object around in the sentence.

Age Appropriateness

Six and older.

Improves

grammar

memory

logical reasoning

Presentation

1. Tell the child a sentence. (EX: The boy was hit by the girl.)

2. Ask him, "What happened in that sentence?"

3. If he answers that the boy hit the girl say, "I'm just going to say the first part of the sentence, "The boy was hit" (pause). Now ask him, "Who got hit?" When he says that the boy got hit say, "Good, now let me finish the sentence, 'by the girl'" (pause). Now ask, "Who hit the boy?"

4. Once you get the right answer, ask him to say the sentence in a different way. (EX) "The girl hit the boy."

List of Thoughts

People were saved by the rescue workers at the site of the earthquake.

Riding down the road, the boy thought of school that day.

Oranges were picked by the farmers on Tuesday.

Blow drying her hair, Mary noticed a new freckle had popped out on her nose and decided she wouldn't talk to her mother that day.

After finishing his dinner, the boy still felt hungry wanting more dessert.

Hitting the puck into the goal, the boy tripped over his stick following the puck into the net.

After chasing the car the exhausted puppy lapped up the water in the gutter.

The family who live next door to my friends will be moving in next door to me as soon as the movers find the truck with their furniture.

Hearing screams, the boy's father came running.

While playing on the beach, the children caught a sand crab.

On Tuesday after the computer lab, we'll take an exam.

After he fell asleep in class, Bill was teased mercilessly by Susan.

Mary once expected Santa to give her a bike.

Roses grow best with a plentiful use of fertilizer.

When Swen gave Scott a tip it seemed to make sense.

The size of your shoes is no indication of your intelligence.

Billabong is the name Australians use for creek.

Happy is the boy with a big jar of candy.

THE CAVEMAN GAME

Goals

To illustrate the symbolic nature of language as individual words and as a complete and meaningful thought.

To intimately understand that speech contains words that can be distinguished by their various functions and used to structure meaning.

To illustrate the basic requirements of a sentence as a complete and meaningful thought.

Age Appropriateness

This activity is appropriate for a child five years old or older.

Improves

    vocabulary

    grammar

    logical reasoning

    creativity

Materials

No special materials are needed.

Presentation

1. Say to the child, "Imagine you're a caveman living in a pre-historic world. People are just beginning to use words to talk about things. Imagine you're with your mom in the woods and a big tiger comes up behind you. You don't see the tiger but your mom does. She shouts **'tiger!'** What do you do?"

2. After she says something along the lines of "run," go on to say, "We believe the first words people learned to use were the names of things. Names are like labels that we use, so that when we say 'tiger' everyone knows exactly what we mean. These labels or names are very useful as you can see from being warned about the tiger. We call this kind of word a noun."

3. Go on to ask, "Now imagine that you're out on your very first hunting trip with your dad and your dad shouts, **'Mammoth!'** Now what do you do?" The child usually says, "run" again. Now say to the child, "That might be a good idea, but cavemen hunted mammoth to eat them and you might have been looking for a mammoth. So you wouldn't want to run away from it. You'd want to kill it. What would you ask your dad if cavemen could use words as well as we do?" The question you want to elicit is, "What should I do?" or something like that.

4. When the child has asked that question say, "We need a new type of word. We need a word that will tell us what to do, what action to take. We call words that show action, verbs. So if your dad were to shout, 'Mammoth... run!' you would know what to do, or if he shouted, 'Mammoth... kill!' you would know what to do."

5. Have the child write a story using only names (nouns) and action words (verbs). It's all right to let them use pronouns if they try to. Children who can't think of anything to write about can be given some direction. A simple idea is to write about what you did that morning, as in the following example.

   I wake. I brush teeth. Mom cooks eggs. I eat eggs. Dad washes dishes. I go school. Teacher write board. I work. I play. I go home. I do lesson Mom.

6. Ask the child if she can understand what she wrote. She may say it's dumb or boring but the point is that it makes sense and a story has been told. It is a good idea to have her practice the writing activity a few times before moving on to the next part of the lesson (you may wait until the next time you work together).

7. Now you tell the child that she is back out with her dad hunting, and he shouts **"tiger run!"** again."What do you do?" The child will likely say "run" again. Say to the child, "What if you run straight into the tiger? What do you need to know so you're sure about exactly what to do?" Keep questioning her until she asks you, "Where is the tiger?" Now say to her, "I need a new type of word to

tell you that, I need a word that tells us the position of the tiger. These types of words we call prepositions. They are words like 'on', 'in' or 'behind'. They tell us where things are, not only physically like, 'the tiger is **on** the rock' but they also tell us where, or when in time something is, like 'the test is **on** Tuesday'. This gives us more information we can use. We can say where and when things are."

8. Now ask the child, "What else do you want to know about the tiger that will help you know what to do?" You are trying to get her to ask questions like, "How big is it?" or, "How strong is it?" You can elicit the questions by asking her things like, "What if it was only a baby tiger, what would you do?" When she asks you a question about the tiger say to her "We need another type of word that describes the tiger, like how big it is, or how fierce it is. This type of word we call an adjective. These are words that give us more information about what things are like."

9. Next you want to have her ask for more information about what the tiger is doing. Ask her questions like, "Does it matter how fast the tiger is moving?" When she wants to know more about how fast the tiger is moving say, "We need another type of word, one that gives us more information about what the tiger is doing. We call these words adverbs. They are words that tell us more about a verb like, 'the tiger is walking **slowly**', or 'the tiger is walking **quickly**'."

10. Ask the child to compare the different effect of the information in these three sentences and ask her how much of a threat the tiger is in each one.

> *A tiger is running at you!*

> *A big, hungry tiger is running quickly straight at you!*

> *A small, cuddly tiger is walking lazily towards you.*

UNDERSTANDING TELLING TOOLS

Goals

To give the child practice understanding that a topic can be written or spoken about using different kinds of tools.

Age Appropriateness

Seven and older.

Materials

You will need paper and pencil for this activity.

Improves

vocabulary

grammar

logical reasoning

creativity

Presentation

1. Choose a topic to tell or write about. You can choose from the Topic List or you can tell about a different topic.

2. If the child is able to read and understand well you should perform this exercise as a reading activity. If he is unable to read with reasonable accuracy you should perform the exercise as an oral activity.

3. Explain that there are many ways to tell about something. Say that first you are going to tell him about your topic by defining it. After definition you can make your way through the following list of telling tools. Do at least two per session so the child has a comparison between telling tools.

Telling Tools

definition

description

quote

example

sequence

categories

cause and effect

fact

what if

anecdote

compare/contrast

Topic List

motorcycles

cars

sports

fun

love

food

friendship

justice

jealousy

fairness

legality

truth

power

rainbows

shrimp

things called Tom

As you progress take time to help the child notice how the different telling tools compare with one another. Also take time to discuss how some telling tools don't work very well with some topics. When this happens, ask the child to think of a topic for which that telling tool may work especially well. Either perform that exercise at the time, or make a note of it for a later activity.

The following is an example of how you might use each of the telling tools on the topic of eggs.

definition- An egg is a natural case that baby animals are in until they are born.

description- Chicken eggs are usually hard on the outside. They can be broken easily. They can be white or light brown. They are about two and a half or three inches by about an inch to an inch and a half. Their shape is ovoid. The inside is clear, wet and sticky, with a yellow middle. If the egg cracks and then no one cleans it up for a day or two, it smells really bad.

example- Eggs are pretty easy to break. If I dropped one from the roof of my house onto my sidewalk it would definitely break, but if an egg rolls off the kitchen table and onto the carpet it might not break.

sequence- Some eggs are good to eat. They should be cooked first. One way to cook an egg is to hard boil it. First you put the egg in a pot. Next you fill the pot until the egg is covered and the water is an inch higher than the egg. Then you put the pot on a high heat until it starts to boil. When the water boils, turn the stove off and cover the pot. Leave the egg in the water for twenty minutes. Cooling the egg is important too. Pour all the water into the sink. Place the pot in the sink and run cool water into the pot for about three minutes. The cool water helps cool the egg without cracking it. Leave the egg sitting in water for at least thirty minutes. Now you can place the egg in the refrigerator. After the egg has chilled for an hour or so it's ready to eat.

parts and categories- There are four parts of a chicken egg. The shell is the hard part on the outside of the egg. The shell membrane is inside the shell. The membrane is soft. It is a thin layer of skin. The egg white is inside the membrane. The white protects the yolk from being damaged. The yolk is inside the white. The yolk is the part of the egg that will turn into a chicken if the egg is fertilized.

compare and contrast- Chicken eggs are not very big. They are smaller than a baseball, but bigger than a jumbo marble. They are not spherical like balls and marbles. They are shaped a little bit like a football. However, unlike a football, they are not the same size at each end. One end comes to a small, round point like a football, but the other end is more rounded like a round ball.

cause and effect- When an egg is inside a mother animal its shell is soft and round, but when it comes out of the mother animal its shell is hard and elongated. The change in the egg is caused by two things. The shape is changed as the egg is pushed out of the mother's body. The egg becomes hard outside the mother's body because it dries in the air.

fact- Eggs are high in protein, which is good for you, but they are also high in fat, which is bad for some people. If you have a heart condition or a gallstone you should not eat many eggs.

what if- If dinosaurs were still on earth they would lay giant eggs. We could use their eggs to feed all the poor and starving people in the world. One dinosaur egg would probably feed about twenty people. But where would we keep the dinosaurs? They could get loose and kill the starving people instead of saving them.

anecdote- I had a friend who told me that he went to a museum and saw a dinosaur egg fossil. He said it was bigger than a football.

quote- My doctor said, "You need more protein. You should have two eggs each day."

TELLING TOOLS

Goals

To give the child practice at describing something in detail.

Age Appropriateness

Seven and older. Don't do this lesson until you have done the lesson Understanding Telling Tools.

Improves

> vocabulary
>
> grammar
>
> logical reasoning
>
> creativity

Presentation

1. Ask the child to think of something and write it down. Have him place the word in a 'mystery envelope'.

2. Now have him tell you about it. Encourage him to use the following telling tools.

> definition
>
> description
>
> example
>
> sequence
>
> categories
>
> comparison and contrast
>
> cause and effect
>
> fact
>
> what if
>
> anecdote
>
> quote

3. Once the child has gotten pretty good at describing things, invite him to describe actions.

USING TELLING TOOLS

Goals

To give the child practice telling about something using different telling tools.

Age Appropriateness

Seven and older. This lesson should not be given before the lesson Understanding Telling Tools.

Improves

vocabulary

grammar

logical reasoning

creativity

Materials

You will need paper and pencil for this activity.

Presentation

1. Invite the child to choose a topic to tell or write about. He can choose from the Topic List or he can tell about a topic of his own.

2. If the child is able he should perform this exercise as a writing activity. If he is unable to write and spell with reasonable accuracy he should perform the exercise as a dictation activity.

3. Explain that there are many ways to tell about something. Say that first you want him to tell about his topic by defining it. After definition you can make your way through the following list of telling tools. You may do one per session and mix in other activities, or you may do two or more per session.

Telling Tools

definition

description

example

sequence

categories

cause and effect

fact

what if

anecdote

quote

Topic List

motorcycles
cars
sports
fun
love
food
friendship
justice
jealousy
fairness
legality
truth
power
rainbows
shrimp
things called Tom

As you progress you should take time to help the child notice how the different telling tools compare with one another. Also take time to discuss how some telling tools don't work very well with some topics. When this happens, ask the child to think of a topic for which that telling tool may work especially well. Either have the child perform that exercise at the time, or make a note of it for a later activity.

4. After compiling the first three or four paragraphs, have the child reread them and start to order them into a composition on the topic. Explain the importance of transitions between paragraphs and invite him to change pieces of the various paragraphs to help them work better together.

PROS AND CONS

Goals

To offer the child practice at making decisions based on multiple variables.

Age Appropriateness

Six years and older.

Improves

    vocabulary

    logical reasoning

    creativity

Materials

Use any set of pros and cons that seems appropriate to a particular student.

Presentation

1. Tell the child that you're going to show him a way to decide what to do. Tell him this is called 'pros and cons'.

2. Explain that 'pro' means 'for' and 'con' means 'against'.

3. Explain that one way to make a decision about something is to list all the 'pros' and all the 'cons' and then make the decision based on these.

4. Ask him to think of a decision he needs to make or one that he has recently made. Use this as the basis of the exercise.

   If he can't think of anything, suggest that you do the exercise with someone else's decision. Think of something relevant to him. EX: "My nephew is trying to decide if he should stay in the public high school he's been attending or move to a private school where he is more likely to make the basketball team."

USING MEANING & CONTEXT

Goals

This activity will help the child understand the relationship between meaning and context.

This activity offers practice revising meaning as you read or listen.

This activity will give the child practice writing meaningful sentences.

Age Appropriateness

This activity is appropriate for a child of six or older.

Improves

vocabulary

grammar

logical reasoning

creativity

Materials

You will need paper and pencil for this activity.

Presentation

1. Tell the child you're going to play a game of finishing sentences. Tell her the first part of the first sentence...

    The boy walked _____.

    ...and then ask her to make up an ending for the sentence and write the whole sentence down. If the child is very young and not very good at writing and spelling, you can write the sentence for her.

2. Now say, "What if the next part was...

    When he got there he went swimming.

What would you add or change about what you made up so that it all makes sense?" Have her write that down too, or write it for her.

3. Continue on with the remaining sentences. Each time you will:

    a. tell her the first part of each sentence

    b. have her finish it

    c. tell her the next sentence

    d. have her adjust it so that the whole thing makes sense

This Saturday is a _____.

I'll bring a gift.

My teacher said _____.

I got an A+.

Sue and Jody went _____.

Then they put it all in the refrigerator.

Do you know _____?

She is a nice girl.

My dog _____.

My mom smacked her with a newspaper.

The farmer _____.

His kids saw it too.

My girlfriend _____.

I broke up with her.

My cat climbed on the _____.

She ate my chicken.

The boat went _____.

I stepped onto the beach.

The girls were _____.

The girls were meeting them there.

I went _____.

I didn't learn a thing.

I want _____.

But I already have three.

Tomorrow is the first day of _____.

I hope my team wins.

Two boys and a girl will _____.

But they don't deserve to.

Before you do the activity again, take a few minutes to develop some new sentences like the ones above.

CLARIFYING AMBIGUITY

Goal

To give the child practice at recognizing and clarifying ambiguity in his reading and writing.

Age Appropriateness

Eight and older.

Improves

vocabulary

grammar

logical reasoning

creativity

Presentation

1. Read one of the ambiguous sentences to the child. (**EX:** The turkey was ready to eat.)

2. Ask him to tell you what it means.

3. If he provides only one meaning, explain that it could also mean something else. Explain the other meaning if he doesn't get it.

4. Invite him to clarify by writing two sentences—one with one meaning and the other with the other meaning. (**EX:** The turkey was ready to be eaten. The turkey was ready to eat his food.)

List of Ambiguous Statements

The turkey is ready to eat.

The steak is rare.

The chicken is done.

The flower (flour) is white.

Sally and Jim had a date.

I feel strange.

That is funny.

He's such a crazy guy.

This is hard.

How do you feel?

Do you have the time?

Time is on your side.

Say that again.

Use stories when these examples are exhausted.

BRAINSTORMING

Goals

To offer the child experiences at exhausting the possibilities as a strategy for problem solving.

When done in couples or a group—to offer practice at cooperating to solve a problem.

Age Appropriateness

Six and older for brainstorming that involves choices only.

(EX) Great names for a big, black dog.

Eight and older for problem solving.

Improves

vocabulary

logical reasoning

creativity

Presentation

1. Explain that you're going to practice coming up with ideas.

2. Tell the child one of the following problems and invite her to come up with ideas to solve it.

3. Some discussion time should be spent explaining why it's important to write these ideas down. Discuss how knowledge can be saved for ourselves and others if we store it in print.

List of Things to Brainstorm

Great names for a big, black dog

Things to do on a rainy day

Uses for a piece of yellow ribbon

Great names for your new bunny

Famous animals you've heard of

Ways to make some extra money

Ways to save time on chores

Favorite movies

Favorite foods

a Christmas list

ideas for Mom's birthday present

sporting events

HEURISTIC PROBLEM SOLVING

Goals

To offer the child experiences at breaking a problem into small parts as a strategy for problem solving.

When done in couples or a group—to offer practice at cooperating to solve a problem.

Age Appropriateness

Nine and older.

Improves

> memory
>
> logical reasoning
>
> creativity

Presentation

1. Explain that you're going to practice solving a problem.

2. Tell the child one of the following problems and invite her to come up with ideas to solve it.

3. Some discussion time should be spent explaining why it's important to write these ideas down. Discuss how knowledge can be saved for ourselves and others if we store it in print.

List of Problems to Solve

You and your friend are on a picnic. You're walking in the woods. You come upon a dog penned in a fence. The dog seems friendly. He begins to whine and bark as if he is hungry. There are no phones around. What can you do?

You are walking along a lake shore. You come upon a rare and beautiful fish you would like to bring back to your aquarium. Your car is parked on the other side of the lake. What can you do?

A truck gets stuck under an overpass. It's blocking traffic. What can the driver do to get it out?

The lights go out during a storm. What are some things you should do?

You're having a party. What do you need to buy?

Your hair dryer stops working and the hair on the right side of your head is still wet. What should you do?

Your coach has dropped you off at home after baseball practice. After she leaves you realize that your parents aren't home. You have no key. It's dark. What should you do?

You and a friend are riding bikes together. You ask him to watch your bike while you go into the store to buy some gum. When you come back, your new bike is all scratched up. Your friend says some punks did it. Who should pay for this? What should you do?

You're hiking with some friends and the strap on your backpack breaks. What should you do?

You and a friend have just finished lunch at Wendy's. You're ready to leave and you realize your purses are missing. What should you do?

You're on a trip. You arrive at the hotel and realize you've got someone else's luggage instead of yours. What should you do?

Your cat is hungry and you don't have any cat food. What should you do?

Use real life when you exhaust these examples.

FALLACIES

Goals

To give the child practice at finding fallacies by understanding their nature.

Age Appropriateness

Nine and older.

Improves

> grammar
>
> logical reasoning
>
> creativity

Presentation

1. Ask the child why the following statement doesn't work.

   (EX) John lives in New York. John has a cold. His cousin Carol lives in North Carolina. She is sick too. I think John caught a cold from Carol.

2. When he tells you what the problem is (EX: "He couldn't have caught a cold from her if they were in two different places") tell him that we call this a 'fallacy of relevance', because it isn't relevant that Carol has a cold.

3. With each new fallacy allow him to tell you the problem, and then tell him the name of the fallacy. Once all the fallacies have been revealed, allow him to decide which kind of fallacy the statement is.

List of Some Common Fallacies Used by Children

irrelevance—see above example.

circumstance—A murder was committed on Friday night when a man was shot with a gun. A gun was found in Sue's trash can on Saturday morning. Therefore Sue is guilty.

argument to the person—Tom wants to go to the beach with Hank. Hank's mom says he can't come. Tom says, "Your mom is mean anyway."

appeal to authority—You're friend tells you that Nike's are the best shoes. He says this is definitely so because Michael Jordan wears them.

universal affirmative—All of the Chicago Bulls are basketball players, therefore all basketball players are Chicago Bulls.

irrelevance—I'll never get an A in Math because my sister always gets one.

circumstance—Somebody robbed the bank last week. Joe once robbed a bank. I'll bet Joe robbed this bank.

authority—Do it because I say so.

universal—John was late to school three times last week. John is always late for school.

USING ELABORATION IN WRITING

Goals

To practice writing elaboratively. To encourage longer written pieces.

Age Appropriateness

Do this lesson with a mature eight year old or an older child. Don't do this lesson until you've done the lesson Guess What.

Improves

> vocabulary
>
> grammar
>
> memory
>
> logical reasoning
>
> creativity

Materials

Use items from the list below.

Presentation

1. Invite the child to choose a topic from the list, or pick one for him.

2. Explain that his assignment is to write a lot about this topic. Tell him you'll give him one point for every word when you grade his work.

List of Topics

> an egg
>
> the inside of a refrigerator
>
> pencil
>
> tooth that fell out
>
> dollar bill
>
> quarter
>
> safety pin

telephone

an insult

blade of grass

leaf

friendship

family

needle

shoe

stopwatch

compass

tea bag

ring

button

locket

sunglasses

Post-it notes

stamp

sparkler

fingernail

golf ball

tweezers

a blank piece of paper

your left nostril

a stuffed animal

ruler

button

HOW-TO EXPOSITORY WRITING

Goals

To offer the child practice writing using description and sequential logic.

To make clear to the child the importance of relaying specific information.

Age Appropriateness

Seven and older.

Improves

vocabulary

grammar

memory

logical reasoning

Materials

You will need paper and pencil for this activity.

Presentation

1. Tell the child that you're going to practice writing about how to do something. Explain that she will need to think of all the steps and that she will need to write about the steps in the correct order.

2. Assign an appropriate choice from the list below.

List of Topics

train a dog to fetch a stick
hard boil an egg
make toast
watch TV
take a shower
eat an apple
get ready for bed
baby-sit
write a 'how to'
make a peanut butter & jelly sandwich

program a VCR
tie shoes
make an ice cream sundae
make a ponytail
wash your hair
get dressed
make a braid
use the internet
start a computer program
ride a bicycle
make a foul shot
cook scrambled eggs
make a paper airplane
plant a seed
roller blade
brush your teeth
take a photograph
wash your hands
polish your nails
build Legos
sing a song
empty the trash
how to stop crying
wait for a bus
do laundry
how to ask someone out on a date
stay out of trouble

USING INFERENCE

Goals

This activity offers practice at determining what we know from a passage and what we don't know, but can surmise or infer.

Age Appropriateness

Seven and older—using stories.

Eight and older—using stories and informative pieces.

Improves

vocabulary

grammar

memory

logical reasoning

creativity

Materials

Start with the examples below.

Add in stories and then informative pieces from books, magazines and newspapers.

Presentation

1. Ask the child to read a passage from the examples below, or any story or informative piece.

2. On a piece of paper, have her list what she certainly knows from this passage.

3. Ask her to list any previous knowledge she brought to the passage that may help her. (EX) The story is about basketball. The star team was down by one point and scored from center court. The story ends without saying who won. Your student knows who won because she has previous knowledge of basketball rules.

4. Now explain that there are certain things we can make an educated guess about based on what we actually know. Generate as many educated questions as possible by questioning her. Explain that the word for this kind of 'educated guessing' is 'surmise'. Explain that when we 'surmise' things we use 'inference'. Say, "For instance if a passage read, 'It was light out, but soon it would be dark,'—we would know from the passage that it is daytime, and that it will be dark soon. We know from previous experience that dark follows light when night falls or an eclipse occurs (if age appropriate). Eclipses occur less frequently than nightfall. We can 'surmise' that it is late afternoon and will soon be nighttime. The writer has 'inferred' this."

List of Paragraphs

The furry beast walked up to the boy. The child trembled. The beast barked.

The wind blew as the boy pulled the rope. The sail would not move.

"When will it be cold enough?" She had cleaned and sharpened her blades two weeks ago. Her impatience permeated all she did.

The bird sat on the feeder. The cat watched. The bird disappeared.

Amy stared out the frosty pane. No school again today. She smiled slightly—and no algebra test either.

Mom and Chuck arrived with the piping hot box just in time to hear my stomach let out a great growl.

As nervous as I am—I'm glad to be having this painful thing pulled.

Use stories when you exhaust these examples.

EXPOSITION USING VISUAL CUES

Goals

To encourage the child to use inference in his assessments.

To encourage the child to write.

Age Appropriateness

Do this lesson with a child who is nine or older and has done the activity Using Inference.

Improves

vocabulary

grammar

memory

logical reasoning

creativity

Materials

You will need pictures from magazines and a pencil and paper.

Presentation

1. Invite the child to study an age appropriate stimulus picture.

2. Ask him to talk about what he can tell for certain about the picture and then what he might surmise about the picture.

3. Ask him if he can add to that and make something up about the picture that would be logically consistent with the scene.

4. Ask him to write a story about the picture.

RESOLVING LOGICAL INCONSISTENCIES

Goals
To offer the child practice at dialectical reasoning.

Age Appropriateness
Eight and older.

Improves
> vocabulary
>
> grammar
>
> memory
>
> logical reasoning

Presentation
1. Tell the child you're going to say something and he needs to figure out why it doesn't make sense.
2. Encourage him to be specific. In the first example below, he should say, "If he drank it <u>all</u>, there <u>isn't</u> any left for breakfast."

List of Inconsistencies
> When Johnny drank all the milk, he left enough for breakfast.
>
> Everyone in the class forgot to bring their homework tomorrow.
>
> Sometimes I never like ice cream.
>
> I always like to do things I hate.
>
> Which way do I go to find the time?
>
> Occasionally Mother and I talk on the phone every day.
>
> His only friend is John and Bob.
>
> We all ate fish since the restaurant had run out of it.
>
> We're late. If you don't hurry up we'll never make it on time.
>
> Why don't you be quiet and say something?

Why can't you see what I'm saying?

I need a haircut because I'm letting my hair grow out.

Do you hear the silence?

What's wrong with being right?

Use your child's illogical statements and those heard on television when you've exhausted these examples.

DEDUCTION JUNCTION

Goals

To show the child the process of deduction. To help her gain experience finding the point (or junction) of deduction.

Age Appropriateness

Eight years and older.

Materials

You will need paper and pencil to record your work.

You may also use pictures from magazines to generate riddles. Choose an interesting picture and make up a riddle about it.

Improves

vocabulary

grammar

memory

logical reasoning

creativity

Presentation

1. Tell the child you're going to tell her a riddle. Explain that she has to solve the riddle. The riddle is: Mike and I went swimming. Mike is a fast swimmer. I didn't swim as well as Mike. Who is the fastest swimmer?

2. Ask the child to solve the riddle. Ask her what words let her know the answer. Repeat the riddle as needed until she can locate the Deduction Junction.

Answer: Mike is the fastest swimmer. Because—Mike is a fast swimmer and I didn't swim as well as Mike did.

3. Offer several riddles and ask the child to find the Deduction Junction in each. If the child is a good reader you should write some of the riddles down and give him practice solving written riddles.

Riddles

Sandy and Bob were hungry. They started to run across the street. A loud noise scared Sandy and she ran back. Who is closer to the candy store—Bob or Sandy?

Answer: Bob is probably closer. Since they were hungry, they were probably running across the street to the candy store. Since Sandy ran back, Bob was closer.

4. Explain that some riddles don't necessarily have a correct answer that you can easily know, but you can make guesses about what's going on.

A dog bit a cat. The dog had to go to the vet. Why?

Maybe—The cat was sick and the dog caught it when he bit the cat.

Or—The dog broke a tooth when he bit the cat.

Or—The dog had to have medicine to make him behave better.

Alternative Presentation

Some older children may be able to generate a riddle or two for you to solve. Magazine pictures are useful for generating riddles from students.

Sam and Charlie were friends. Charlie and Bob were friends. Who probably didn't play together?

It was a very odd day. It was 85 degrees. It was very hot for this time of year. What season was it?

I'm afraid of heights, so I hold on tight. The leaves are making me itchy. Where am I?

The sun turned black. What was happening?

I'm floating. I'm wet. Where am I?

I'm a tiny creature. My wings beat very quickly. I'm not an insect. What am I?

I have wings and a nose and a tail. I can fly. I'm not alive. What am I?

I can run. I can be cold or hot. I can make myself invisible. What am I?

WORD SANDWICHES

Goals

To offer the child practice at linking word symbols in a meaningful way.

Age

Six years or older.

Improves

vocabulary

grammar

logical reasoning

creativity

Presentation

1. Tell the child that you're going to tell him two words and you'd like him to use them in a sentence.

2. Start by having him tell you the sentence and you can write it down for him. When he's able, have him write the sentence.

Word List

cramp—lagoon

snip—lobster

gladly—crunch

saddle—dog

please—grind

share—random

smoke—grow

cringe—pretty

crab—pinch

hot—mice

madly—happen

open—chalkboard

sniff—paper

simply—happily

turn—stop

glow—running

listen—sleep

stapler—picture

lamp—stamp

pick—don't

net—spoon

ground—chair

microscope—Asia

lost—table

telephone—roof

stand—caution

virtue—rice

bandage—goggles

delivery—poem

3. When the child has gotten pretty good at this activity give him sets of phrases to make into one sentence.

FAST TALK

Goals

To develop the ability to react quickly to a topic and to formulate one's thoughts and then speak them in a coherent way.

To get used to speaking formally as one writes.

To prepare for a more formal public speaking format.

Age

Six and older.

Improves

vocabulary

grammar

memory

logical reasoning

creativity

Materials

The topics below and any others you want to add, written on a piece of paper and put into a can for drawing from.

Something to time yourselves with.

Presentation

1. Invite the child to play a game of fast talking. Tell him you'll take turns drawing from the can and then talking for one minute on the topic drawn. Tell him that the rules are that the speaker should try to talk in complete sentences like those we see in books.

2. Start the activity by drawing first so you can demonstrate.

3. Give him a turn.

   Increase the required talk time as the child gets better at this activity.

List of Topics

    stuffed animals

    grapes

    snowboarding

    dentists

    dirt

    Valentine's Day

    trees

    canoeing

    rain forests

    Italy

    volcanoes

    pencils

    things called Tom

    weather

    boots

    basketball

    paper clips

    cameras

    zebras

    books

    a movie you just saw

    the internet

    orange juice

JUST THE FACTS

Goals

To improve the child's ability to recognize facts from inference and lies.

Age

Seven years or older.

Materials

Age appropriate books, magazines and newspapers.

Paper and a pencil.

Improves

    logical reasoning

Presentation

1. Have the child read an appropriate passage from a book, magazine or newspaper.

2. Ask him what we can tell to be a fact, or the truth, in the story, as opposed to what is not true, or what we don't know to be true.

3. Ask him to make a list of facts.

4. Discuss how he could tell that these were facts.

INTERACTIVE WRITING

Goals

To increase the length, complexity, thoroughness, and overall quality of written
work.

Age

Age nine or older.

Materials

Paper and pencil.

A folder for sending work back and forth.

(or) Two computers with internet access.

Improves

vocabulary

grammar

memory

logical reasoning

creativity

Presentation

1. Invite the child to write a piece for you on any topic of your or his choice. If
you both have a computer and internet access it can be fun and add more interest for the child to write it on-line and e-mail it to you. If not, you'll need a
folder or envelope for sending the piece back and forth.

2. Read the piece. Develop a few questions based on what the child has written.
These questions should be intended to make the piece better and longer. Send
the piece and the questions back to the child.

3. Have him answer the questions by fitting them in wherever he'd like in the
piece. Then he should send it back to you.

4. Make suggestions regarding the additions and ask more questions.

5. Carry on like this until the piece is quite long and in a logical order.

WORD ORIENTATION

Goals

To cause the child to act upon the word in a meaningful way, thereby formalizing it as part of his personal schema.

Age

Seven years or older.

Materials

Paper and a pencil

An age appropriate dictionary.

Improves

vocabulary

grammar

logical reasoning

creativity

Presentation

1. Choose a word from the first list (EX) sparkplug. Tell the child that he needs to write a sentence about this word in relation to each of the words in the second list. (EX)

size	A spark plug is about two inches long.
shape	A spark plug is two inches long and about a half inch around.
niceness	A spark plug is nice to have because it starts your car.
generosity	A spark plug is generous because it shares energy with your car.
	...Carry on with the entire list.

Alternative Presentation

1. Choose a word from list two and have the child write about it in relation to each word in list one.

(EX) agility

A piano is not very agile. It is heavy and can't move on its own.

A cat is agile, leaping as high as five or six feet.

etc....

List One

size

niceness

generosity

playfulnes

diligence

hardness

friendliness

objectivity

speed

smoothness

agility

longevity

Add vocabulary words or any new word.

List Two

cat

piano

bread

spark plug

zebra

can opener

EXCLAMATION POINT!

Goals

To get the child used to noticing the places where the marks would be in spoken language.

Age

Six and older.

Materials

A piece of paper or poster board with the punctuation marks you're teaching written in bold marker.

For classroom use have each child make a replica of the punctuation marks you're working on on black poster board. These can be glued or stapled to a popsicle stick. The children can hold these up at appropriate times.

Improves

grammar

logical reasoning

Presentation

1. Explain briefly what the markings are for.

2. Have a piece of paper or poster board on the table with the marks you're teaching written in bold marker on the paper.

3. Ask the child to point to the appropriate mark at the appropriate time.

4. Using a lot of intonation, read to the child from a book.

AFTERWORD

According to Albert Bandura, "Human nature is characterized by a vast potentiality that can be fashioned by direct and observational experience into a variety of forms within biological limits." This is our challenge, as parents, as teachers and as the students who they love so dearly—*to fulfill the human potential*. This is no small task. It weighs heavily on us all. But heavy though it may be, it needs must be heavier still—heavier and heavier until we are so burdened that we can progress no further without alas getting it right. As we write these final words we are filled with awe that they will come to print in the next millennium—the age of wonder? The promised land? The time that our parents promised would be better still than the days of our youth. What such promises can we make to our children? We must answer this and many more questions. We must deliver to them at least the potential for greatness. These dreams that our parents had for us, do we dream them for our children? Do we even know how? Can we even conceive of what to dream? We live in an age in which everything we survey is open to re-definition. As we go about our lives, running businesses and school car pools, cooking dinner, golfing and paying bills, we are preparing our children for careers we cannot even conceive of. And we scarcely have a free moment to give. We are both the winners of bread and other niceties, and the creators of tomorrow, brighter still than today? What fruit will our effort bear? This is up to us—to you, to me, to us all. We have no room for error. Only right choices can be made. In a world of instant everything, we have but a decade or two to get these children right, these babies that have fallen from the stars into our lives—the parents of our grandchildren. The writers of the future of our planet, and likely other planets too.

My father died twenty years ago at the age of sixty-three to a disease that is largely curable today. At forty-three, I've not yet seen my *mid-life* according to statistics, our daughter Amanda will live to be one hundred years of age, and likely not get a post card from the President as this will be no great feat in 2083. Her golden years will be from eighty to one hundred! My father predicted this, as did yours. A better time. Longer life. He said we would have to invent a new season, to re-write the Sinatra song about the seasons of our lives. Dad saw most things in life through the words of a song. Though he couldn't read musical notation, he kept the sheet music perched high atop his piano as he played—by ear, hoping that one day the pieces would fit together and the mystery would come clear, the code would come into focus. It would have done, I'm sure—had he lived long enough. Played enough Lennon and McCartney, Sinatra. What will fill Amanda's days, the season yet unnamed? What gifts can we, a man and woman of the 1900s, give to a child of tomorrow? What—when we have so little time in which to give it. The smallest part of a decade or two? So many things come to mind—so many needs, so much to be done. But which of them will answer the challenges of her life when we are gone? Which of them will fill her golden years, the season yet unnamed, with wonder still, as her hair grows grey alas at ninety-four? Wonder! Wonder is all we have to give. Wonder enough for her to save some for her own children. This is what we leave to our little ones— *wonder!* And the reason to solve all that they can imagine.

—Carmen McGuinness

REFERENCES

Honzik, M. P., McFarlane, J. W., & Allen, L. 1948. The stability of mental test performance between two and eighteen years. *Journal of Experimental Education, 17,* 309-323.

Sears, R. R., Maccoby, E. E., & Levin, H. 1957. *Patterns of Child Rearing.* New York: Harper & Row.

Baumrind, D. 1971. Harmonious parents and their preschool children. *Developmental Psychology, 4(1),* 99-102.

Baumrind, D. 1979. *Sex Related Socialization Effects.* Paper presented at the biannual meeting of the Society for Research in Child Development, San Francisco.

Cattell, R. B. 1965. *The Scientific Analysis of Personality.* Baltimore: Penguin Books.

Flavell, J. 1963. *The Developmental Psychology of Jean Piaget.* New York: Van Nostrand.

Flavell, J. 1966. Role-taking and communication skills in children. *Young Childen 21(3)* 164-177.

Montessori, M. 1967. *The Absorbent Mind (2nd ed.).* New York: Dell Publishing.

Baldwin, A. 1968. *Theories of Child Development*. New York: Wiley.

Maslow, A. 1954. *Motivation and Personality*. New York: Harper & Row.

Juel, C., Griffith, P. and Gough, P. 1986. Acquisition of literacy: A longitudinal study of children in first and second grade. *Journal of Educational Psychology*, 78, 243-55.

Perkins, D. 1994. *Knowledge as Design*. Pacific Grove, California: Critical Thinking Press and Software.

Perkins, D. 1996. *Outsmarting IQ*. New York: Free Press.

Boden, M. 1996. "What is Creativity". In M. Bowden (Ed.), *Dimensions of Creativity*. Cambridge: MIT Press, 75-117.

Koestler, A. 1996. The Act of Creation. London: Hutchinson.

Hesse, M. B. 1988. "Theories, Family Resemblances, and Analogies". In D. H. Helman (Ed.), *Analogical Reasoning*. Amsterdam: Kluwer, 317-340.

Flavell, J. H., Beach, D. R. and Chinsky, J. M. 1966. Spontaneous verbal rehearsal in a memory task as a function of age. *Child Development*, 37, 283-299.

Moely, B. E., Olsen, F. A., Halwes, T. G. and Flavell, J. H. 1969. Production deficiency in young children's clustered recall. *Developmental Psychology*, 1, 26-34.

Schneider, W. 1986. The role of conceptual knowledge and metamemory in the development of organizational principles in memory. *Journal of Experimental Child Psychology*, 42, 318-336.

Ceci, S. J. and Howe, M. J. A. 1978. Age related differences in recall as a function of retrieval flexibility. *Journal of Experimental Child Psychology*, 26, 432-442.

Daneman, M. and Carpenter, P. A. 1980. Individual differences in working memory and reading. *Journal of Verbal Learning and Verbal Behavior*, 19, 450-466.

Craik, F. I. M. and Tulving, E. 1975. Depth of processing and the retention of words in episodic memory. *Journal of Experimental Psychology, 104*, 268-294.

Craik, F. I. M. 1977. 'A level of analysis' view of memory. In P. Pliner, L. Krames T. M. Allaway (Eds.), *Communication and Affect*, Vol. 2: *Language and Thought*. New York: Academic Press.

Craik, F. I. M. and Lockhart, R. S. 1972. Levels of processing a framework for memory research. *Journal of Verbal Learning and Verbal Behavior, 11*, 671-684.

Graf, P. and Schacter, D. L. 1985. Implicit and explicit memory for new associations in normal and amnesic subjects. *Journal of Experimental Psychology: Learning, Memory and Cognition, 13*, 45-53.

Russo, R. and Parkin, A. J. 1993. Age differences in implicit memory, *Memory and Cognition*.

Light, L. L. and Carter-Sobell, L. 1970. Effects of changed semantic context on recognition memory. *Journal of Verbal Learning and Verbal Behavior*, 9, 1-11.

Ryle, G. 1949. *The Concept of Mind*. London: Hutchinson.

Cuvo, A. J. 1974. Incentive level influence on overt rehearsal and free recall as a function of age. *Journal of Experimental Child Psychology, 19*, 265-278.

Tulving, E. 1985. How many memory systems are there? *American Psychologist, 40*, 385-398.

Squire, L. R. 1992. *Encyclopedia of Learning and Memory*. New York: Macmillan.

Davidson, J. E., Deuset, R. and Sternberg, R. J. 1994. "The role of metacognition in problem solving". In J. Metcalfe and A. P. Shimamura (Eds.), *Metacognition: Knowing About Knowing*, 207-226. Cambridge: MIT Press.

Glaser, R. and Chi, M. T. H. 1988. Overview. In M. T. H. Chi, R. Glaser and M. J. Farr (Eds.), *The Nature of Expertise*. xv-xxxvi. Hillsdale, NJ: Erlbaum.

Donley, R. D. and Ashcraft, M. H. 1992. The methodology of testing naive beliefs in the physics classroom. *Memory and Cognition*, 381-391.

Mayer, R. E. 1982. "The psychology of mathematical problem solving". In F. K. Lester and J. Garofalo (Eds.), *Mathematical Problem Solving Issues in Research*, 1-13. Philadelphia: The Franklin Institute.

Mayer, R. E. 1995. "Implications of cognitive psychology for instruction in mathematical problem solving". In E. A. Silver (Ed.), *Teaching and Learning Mathematical Problem Solving*, 123-138. Hillsdale, NJ: Erlbaum.

Keane, M. T. 1988. *Analogical problem solving*. Chichester, Great Britain: Ellis Horwood.

Lawson, D. L. and Lawson, A. E. 1993. Neural principles of memory and a neural theory of analogical insight. *Journal of Research on Science Thinking*, 30, 1327-1348.

Halpern, D. F., Hansen, C. and Riefer, D. 1990. Analogies and an aid to understanding and memory. *Journal of Educational Psychology*, *82*, 298-305.

Holyoak, K. J. and Koh, K. 1987. Surface and structural similarity in analogical transfer. *Memory and Cognition*, *15*, 332-340.

Reed, S. K. 1993 A schema based theory of transfer. In D. K. Detterman and R. J. Sternberg (Eds.), *Transfer On Trial: Intelligence, Cognition, and Instruction*, 39-67. Norwood, NJ: Ablex.

McClelland, D. C. 1987. *Human Motivation*, Cambridge, MA: Cambridge University Press.

Mehribian, A. and Ksionzky, S. *A Theory of Affiliation*. Lexington, MA: Heath, 1974.

Sorrentino, R. M. and Sheppard, B. H. 1978. Effects of affiliation-related motives on swimmers in individual versus group competition: A field experiment. *Journal of Personality and Social Psychology, 36,* 704-714.

Frisch, D. and Clemen, R. T. 1994. Beyond expected utility: Rethinking behavioral decision research. *Psychological Bulletin, 116,* 46-54.

Dunker, K. 1945. On problem solving. *Psychological Monographs, 58,* (Whole No. 270).

Smyth, M. M., Collins, A. F., Morris, P. E. and Levy, P. 1994. *Cognition in Action (2nd ed.)* Hove, Great Britain: Erlbaum.

Evans, J. St. B. T. 1993. The cognitive psychology of reasoning: An introduction. *The Quarterly Journal of Experimental Psychology, 46A,* 561-567.

Piaget, Jean. 1981. *The Psychology of Intelligence* (9th ed.). Totowa, NJ: Littlefield, Adams & Co.

Chomsky, N. 1957. *Syntax Structures.* The Hague: Mouton.

Chomsky, N. 1965. *Aspects of Theory of Syntax.* Cambridge, MA: MIT Press.

McCloskey, M., Caramazza, A. and Green, B. 1980. Curvilinear motion in the absence of external forces: Naive beliefs about the motion of objects. *Science, 210,* 1139-1141.

Case, R. 1974. Structures and strictures: Some functional limitations on the course of cognitive growth. *Cognitive Psychology*, 6, 544-577.

Wason, P. C. and Johnson-Laird, P. N. 1972. *Psychology of Reasoning: Structure and Content.* Cambridge, MA: MIT Press.

Salmon, M. H. 1991. "Informal reasoning and informal logic". In J. F. Voss, D. N. Perkins and J. W. Segal (Eds.), *Informal Reasoning and Education*, 153-168. Hillsdale, NJ: Erlbaum.

Arlin, P. K. 1980. *Adolescent and adult thought: A search for structures.* Paper presented at meetings of the Piaget Society. Philadelphia, PA.

Allport, G. W. 1937. *Personality: A Psychological Interpretation.* New York: Holt.

Brown, S. L., Walter, M. I. 1990. *The art of problem posing* (2nd ed.). Hillsdale, NJ: Erlbaum.

Henessey, B. A. 1994. "Finding (and solving?) the problem" [Review of problem finding, problem solving and creativity]. *Contemporary Psychology*, 40, 971-972.

Thomas, J. C. 1989. "Problem Solving by Human-Machine Interaction". In K. J. Gilhooly (Ed.), *Human and Machine Problem Solving*, 317-362.

Deci, E. L. 1975. *Intrinsic Motivation.* New York: Plenum.

Warrington, E. K. and Ackroyd, C. 1975. The effects of orienting tasks on recognition memory. *Memory and Cognition, 3,* 140-142.

Meacham, J. A. and Singer, J. 1977. Incentive in prospective remembering. *Journal of Psychology, 97,* 191-197.

Meacham, J. A. 1982. A note on remembering to execute planned actions. *Journal of Applied Developmental Psychology, 3,* 121-133.

Waughn, N. C. and Norman, D. A. 1965. Primary memory. *Psychological Review, 72,* 89-104.

Schneider, W. and Schiffrin, R. M. 1977. Controlled and automatic information processing. *Psychological Review, 84,* 1-66.

Birch, L.L., Marlin, D.W., and Rotter, J. 1984. Eating as the "means" activity in a contingency: Effects on young children's food preference. *Child Development, 55,* 431-439.

Lepper, M.R. and Greene, D. 1975. Turning play into work: Effects of adult surveillance and extrinsic rewards on children's motivation. *Journal of Personality and Social Psychology, 31,* 479-486.

Lepper, M.R. and Greene, D. 1978. "Overjustification Research and Beyond: Toward a Means-ends Analysis of Intrinsic and Extrinsic Motivation". In M.R. Lepper and D. Greene (Eds.), *The Hidden Costs of Reward.* Hillsdale, NJ: Erlbaum.

deCharms, R. and Carpenter, V. 1968. "Measuring motivation in culturally disadvantaged school children". In H. J. Klausmeirer and G. T. O'Hearn (Eds.), *Research and Development Toward the Improvement of Education.* Madison, WI: Educational Research Services.

Weiner, B. A. 1980. A cognitive (attribution)-emotion-action model of motivated behavior: An analysis of judgements of help-giving. *Journal of Personality and Social Psychology, 39,* 186-200.

deCharms, R. and Muir, M. S. 1978. Motivation: Social approaches. *Annual Review of Psychology, 29,* 91-113.

Perlmutter, L. C., Scharff, K., Karsh, R. and Monty, R. A. 1980. Perceived control: A generalized state of motivation. *Motivation and Emotion, 4,* 35-45.

Chanowitz, B. and Langer, E. 1982. "Knowing More (or Less) Than You Can Show: Understanding Control Through the Mindlessness-Mindfulness Distinction". In M. E. P. Seligman and J. Garber (Eds.), *Human Helplessness*. New York: Academic Press.

Bandura, A. 1982. Self efficacy mechanism in human agency. *American Psychologist, 37*, 122-147.

Bandura, A. 1985. "Model of Causality in Social Learning Theory". In M. J. Mahoney and A. Freeman (Eds.), *Cognition and Psychotherapy*. New York: Plenum.

Ekman, P. 1971. 1972. "Universal and Cultural Differences in Facial Expressions of Emotion". In J. K. Cole (Ed.), *Nebraska Symposium on Motivation*. Lincoln: University of Nebraska Press.

Lewis, C. C. 1981. The effects of parental firm control: a reinterpretation of findings. *Psychological Bulletin, 90*, 547-563.

Bower, G. H. 1981. Mood and memory, *American Psychologist, 36*, 129-148.

Perrig, W. J. and Perrig, P. 1988. Mood and memory: Mood congruity effects in the absence of mood. *Memory and Cognition, 16*, 102-109.

Berko Gleason, J. 1989. Studying Language Development. In J. Berko Gleason (Ed.), *The Development of Language*. Columbus: Merrill.

Pinker, S. 1994. *The Language Instinct*. New York: Morrow.

Dunn, L.M. and Peabody, L.M. 1981. *Peabody Picture Vocabulary Test— Revised*. Circle Pines, MN: American Guidance Service.

Atchison, J. 1987. *Words in the Mind: An Introduction to the Mental Lexicon*. London: Blackwell.

Brown, R. and Berko, J. 1960. Word association and the acquisition of grammar. *Child Development, 31*, 1-14.

Brown, R. 1968. *Words and Things.* New York: Free Press.

Penner, S. 1987. Parental responses to grammatical and ungrammatical child utterances. *Child Development, 58*, 376-384.

Best, D. L. and Ornstein, P.A. 1986. Children's generation and communication of mnemonic organizational strategies. *Developmental Psychology, 22*, 845-853.

DeLoache, J.S., Cassidy, D.J. and Brown, A.L. 1985. Precursors of mnemonic strategies in very young children. *Child Development, 56*, 125-137.

Flavell, J.H. and Wellman, H.M. 1977. Metamemory. In R.V. Kail and J. Hagen (Eds.), *Memory in Cognitive Development.* Hilldale, NJ: Erlbaum.

Cole, M. and Scribner, S. 1977. Cross-cultural Studies of Memory and Cognition. In R.V. Kail and J. Hagen (Eds.), *Memory in Cognitive Development.* Hillsdale, NJ: Erlbaum.

Reber, A.S. 1992. Implicit learning and tacit knowledge. *Journal of Experimental Psychology, 118*, 219-235.

Berry, D.C. and Dienes, Z. 1993. *Implicit and Explicit Learning in Human Performance.* Hillsdale, NJ: Erlbaum.

Berry, D.C. and Broadbent, D.E. 1988. Interactive tasks and the implicit-explicit distinction. *British Journal of Psychology, 79*, 251-272.

Nelson, K. 1973. Structure and strategy in learning to talk. *Monographs of the Society for Research in Child Development, 38*.

Nelson, K. 1978. Semantic Development and the Development of Semantic Memory. In K.E. Nelson (Ed.), *Children's Language.* New York: Gardner Press.

Clark, E.V. 1973. What's in a Word? On the Child's Acquisition of Semantics in his First Language. In T.E. Moore (Ed.), *Cognitive Development and the Acquisition of Language.* Orlando, FL: Academic Press.

Clarkson, M.G. and Berg, W.K. 1983. Cardiac orientation and vowel discrimination in newborns: Crucial stimulus parameters. *Child Development, 54,* 162-171.

De Boysson-Bardies, B., Sagart, L. and Durand, C. 1984. Discernible differences in the babbling of infants according to target language. *Journal of Child Language, 11,* 1-16.

Carey, S. and Bartlett, E. 1978. Acquiring a single new word. *Papers and Reports on Child Language Development, 15,* 17-29.

Bohannon, J.N. and Warren-Leubecker, A. 1985. Theoretical Approaches to Language Acquisition. In J. Berko Gleason (Ed.), *The Development of Language.* Westerville, OH: Merrill.

Reich, P.A. 1986. *Language Development.* Englewood Cliffs, NJ: Erlbaum.

McNeill, D. 1970. *The Acquisition of Language.* New York: Harper and Row.

Brown, R. 1973. *A First Language: The Early Stages.* Cambridge, MA: Harvard University Press.

Berko, J. 1958. The child's learning of English morphology. *Word, 14,* 150-177.

Slobin, D.I. 1979. *Psycholinguistics.* Glenview, IL: Scott, Foresman.

Dale, P.S. 1976. *Language Development Structure and Function.* New York: Holt, Rinehart and Winston.

Bloom, L., Merkin, S. and Wootten, J. 1982. Wh-questions: Linguistic factors that contribute to the sequence of acquisition. *Child Development, 53,*

1084-1092.

de Villiers, P.A. and de Villiers, J.G. 1979. *Early Language.* Cambridge, MA: Harvard University Press.

Shatz, M. and Gelman, R. 1973. The development of communication skills: Modifications in the speech of young children as a function of the listener. *Monographs of the Society for Research in Child Development, 38* (Serial No. 152).

McCall, R.B., Applebaum, M.I. and Hogarty, P.S. 1973. Developmental changes in mental test performance. *Monographs of the Society for Research in Child Development, 38*(3, Serial No. 150).

McClelland, D.C. and Pilon, D.A. 1983. Sources of adult motives in patterns of behavior in early childhood. *Journal of Personality and Psychology, 44(3),* 564-574.

McGuinness, C., McGuinness, D. and McGuinness, G. 1996. Phono-Graphix: A new method for remediating reading difficulties. *Orton Annals of Dyslexia, 46,* 73-96.

McGuinness, C. and McGuinness, G. 1998. *Reading Reflex.* New York: Free Press.

OECD and Statistics Canada. 1997. *Literacy Skills for the Knowledge Society.*

NAEP 1994. *Reading Report Card for the Nation and States.* 1996. Office of Educational Research and Improvement. US Department of Education.

PROGRAM EVALUATION